CHOREOGRAPHY AND DANCE

GV 1785. J57
DAN

Editor in Chief
Robert P. Cohan CBE

Associate Editor for USA
Muriel Topaz

Associate Editor for Germany
Rolf Garske

Advisory Editors for the UK
David Dougill, Alastair Macaulay

Advisory Editor for France
Jean Claude Dienis

Aims and Scope

Choreography and Dance: An International Journal is concerned with the composition of ballet and related forms of dance performed on stage. The journal covers the techniques and training of choreographers, and the development of choreography together with historical, social, folk and other influences on dance. It will also cover its relationship with other components of dance performance such as music and lighting, and the work and influence of individual choreographers. The journal will compare and contrast dance forms worldwide, using dance notation and video to facilitate analysis.

Notes for contributors can be found at the back of the journal.

© 1993 Harwood Academic Publishers GmbH. All rights reserved.
Reprinted 2004
by Routledge,
2 Park Square, Milton Park, Abingdon, Oxon OX14 4RN

Transferred to Digital Printing 2004

Ordering Information

Each volume is comprised of an irregular number of parts depending upon size. Issues are available individually as well as by subscription. 1993 Volumes: 2–4

Orders may be placed with your usual supplier or directly with Harwood Academic Publishers GmbH in care of the addresses shown on the inside back cover. Journal subscriptions are sold on a per volume basis only. Claims for nonreceipt of issues will be honored free of charge if made within three months of publication of the issue. Subscriptions are available for microform editions; details will be furnished upon request.

All issues are dispatched by airmail throughout the world.

Subscription Rates

Base list subscription price per volume: ECU 53.00 (US $63.00).* This price is available only to individuals whose library subscribes to the journal OR who warrant that the journal is for their own use and provide a home address for mailing. Orders must be sent directly to the Publisher and payment must be made by personal check or credit card.

Separate rates apply to academic and corporate institutions. These rates may also include photocopy license and postage and handling charges. Special discounts are available to continuing subscribers through our Subscriber Incentive Plan (SIP).

*ECU (European Currency Unit) is the worldwide base list currency rate; payment can be made by draft drawn on ECU currency in the amount shown or in local currency at the current conversion rate. The US Dollar rate is based on the ECU rate and applies to North American subscribers only. Subscribers from other territories should contact their agents or one of the offices listed on the inside back cover.

(Continued on inside back cover)

(Continued from inside front cover)

To order direct and for enquiries, contact:

Europe
Y-Parc, Chemin de la Sallaz
1400 Yverdon, Switzerland
Telephone (024) 239-670
Fax: (024) 239-671

Far East (excluding Japan)
Kent Ridge, PO Box 1180
Singapore 9111
Telephone: 741-6933
Fax: 741-6922

USA
PO Box 786, Cooper Station
New York, N.Y. 10276
Telephone: (212) 206-8900
Fax: (212) 645-2459

Japan
Yohan Western Publications Distribution Agency
3-14-9, Okubo, Shinjuku-ku, Tokyo 169, Japan
Telephone: (03) 3208-0181
Fax: (03) 3209-0288

Distributed by STBS - Publishers Distributor

Choreography and Dance
1993, Vol. 3, Part 2, pp. 1-6
Photocopying permitted by license only

The times that gave birth to Kurt Jooss

Walter Sorell

The turn of the century when Kurt Jooss was born was marked by cultural decadence. The artists sought change and the search for new directions gave birth to new creative expressions. Germany was in the forefront of the creative explosion of the 1920's. In dance of the visionary teacher Rudolf Laban emphasized a new awareness of space and a new movement-consciousness. He was the greatest influence on the artistic development of his pupil Kurt Jooss. Later on Jooss found inspiration in the political writings of Kurt Tucholsky, the major contributor to the magazine *Die Weltbuhne*. Both Tucholsky and Jooss had a sense of foreboding at the approaching disaster of the next world war.

KEY WORDS   Rudolf Laban, Kurt Tucholsky, *Die Weltbuhne*, Weimar Republic, Mary Wigman, *The Green Table*

When Kurt Jooss was born, our century made its very first step into history. The year was 1901. When he was still an infant the flowery, playful Jugendstil dominated the scene, but at the same time there was a noticeable tendency to escape reality. The turn of the century was a decadent period in which one drowned one's emptiness and despair in a happy cancanization of life. Politically there was a feeling of deadly satiation. The world was fully colonized, its riches unevenly distributed. History moved in unbalanced righteousness toward inevitable conflicts.

The artists sought to save the skin of their minds. Gauguin fled the sterility of bourgeois life, calling the world he left behind more barbarian than the imaginary regained paradise on Tahiti. Isadora Duncan freed herself from the fetters of classic ballet, but not without giving the romanticism of the past a new glaze. Ruth St. Denis escaped to the East and wedded the spirit of Tao with the sermon on the mount. With her Indian dances she delighted the Europeans who thirsted for a different life and eagerly accepted any facsimile of their dreams of the East. Such novelists as Pierre Loti fashioned heroes who sought relief from the perplexities of their psyche, and in their rebellion against the past and its norms they fled into the wilderness of the unknown.

The search for man's identity was the moving force behind most artistic manifestations, particularly in the first two decades of this century. Battle cries accompanied this search, and the "isms" mushroomed to the accompaniment of Schoenberg's atonal sounds: Fauvism, cubism, vorticism, symbolism, expressionism, futurism, dadaism, constructivism, surrealism. Between Ezra Pound's "Make it new!" and John Cage's "Let's start from scratch!" lie one shock of the new after another. Early in the century Georges Braque had said that "art is made to disturb." Paul Klee expressed the artists' need to return to the beginning with the words, "I want to be as new born, knowing no pictures, entirely without impulses, almost in an original state." André Malraux summed it all up in declaring that "all art is a revolt against man's fate." In no previous epoch had the artist so dissociated himself from the society to which he belonged and for which he supposedly created. Aldous Huxley acknowledged this when he said, "art is no longer one of the means whereby man seems to redeem a life which is experienced as chaotic, senseless and largely evil."

There was one other "ism," not well defined in the public consciousness, but of the greatest importance for the development of all the arts in the twentieth century. I call it "surprisism." In 1912 Jean Cocteau concocted the ballet *Le Dieu Bleu*, characteristic of past romantic conceits. It was a stunning flop, and thereafter Diaghilev ignored Cocteau. Cocteau, who was far more accustomed to praise, questioned Diaghilev about his reserve, and it was then, on Place de la Concorde, that Diaghilev uttered the historic words: "Étonne-moi!" Surprise me! It has become the slogan of our time.

Diaghilev himself had surprised the world when he opened his first of twenty seasons in Paris in 1909. In describing his success, Cocteau said that "he splashed Paris with colours!" But Diaghilev did more than that. When he arrived on the scene the art of ballet was in a poor state. The words "sterile" and "stereotypic" would best describe its artistic level. Diaghilev's productions employed the greatest dancers, choreographers, composers and stage designers. He dared to present controversial material in a controversial manner, and thrived on theatrical scandals that later became renowned successes: *Afternoon of a Faun, Sacre du Printemps, Parade*. He gave twentieth century ballet a new lease on life.

When Isadora undertook to do battle against ballet at the beginning of the century, a spiritual force was set free, fighting for a new freedom of the dancing body, all feeling in motion. There was an endearing, passionate soul afloat, looking for a body. In 1913, on Monte Verità, a fascinating man named Rudolf Laban began to fashion dancing bodies. He taught rhythmic movement, or what he loosely labelled free dancing. He was a man of magnetic power, his eyes afire with a vision. In those early years of his career he was always seen with his notation papers or with a drum in his hand, inventing movement, experimenting, improvising.

One of his most accomplished students, Mary Wigman, saw in him "the magician, the priest of an unknown religion, the worshipped hero, the lord of a dreamlike and yet ever-so-real kingdom." At that time the dancer envisioned by Laban was not yet born. He had to build up this new bodily instrument. In doing so he caught the spirit of the would-be dancer and set him artistically free. Laban had the extraordinary quality of enabling each one to find his or her own roots, of discovering his own potentialities and the technique that fitted body and mind, an individual style of dancing. In such manner, Laban fulfilled Isadora Duncan's dream of the new free dancer, finding the right body for its soul.

Mary Wigman created dances that were no longer trying to shape a very personal feeling, an emotional experience only, as was Isadora's language. She wanted to reach her audiences with a message that had universal meaning. She aimed at the dramatic interpretation of the conflicts within the individual and in relation to the influence of the outside world. She asked for substance, for some significance in her body's speech. She felt that the dance she wanted to create had to be born out of necessity.

What happened in Germany during and after the First World War in the dance field was either balletic, gymnastic, or a kind of pretty-pretty dance, like the Danube waltzes in which the Wiesenthal sisters waltzed themselves into fame. It was entirely characteristic of the era that a great deal of the dancing was done in the nude in nightclubs. The star of those dancers was Anita Berber, who also loved to be seen at receptions and in theatres covered only by a fur coat.

The German audiences were used to this variety of dancing, not to anything so serious as Mary Wigman's masked *Witch Dance* or her ecstatic dances of prayer and sacrifice, presented in an almost defiant manner by a dancer who was neither young nor pretty. Between 1914 and 1920 she had little success, was misunderstood and often booed. It was only in the early 1920's that her dance works were recognized as a vital contribution to the expressionism then current, an art form never seen before, bewildering and sometimes frightening in its subject matter. Whatever she danced was the mirror image of her time, and became known as the German Ausdruckstanz.

When we look back at the 1920's from our vantage point, we see that they were unique on both sides of the ocean. Nonetheless, the most decisive artistic changes and the strongest cultural impulses came from Germany. The phenomenon of a defeated nation rising to singular artistic greatness is reflected in the epithets we use to label those years: Americans speak of their "roaring twenties," while Germans know them as their "golden years."

This explosion of creativity happened at a time of the greatest difficulty in every sector of human existence. But in spite of the daily fight for survival, the madness of political divisions, and a haunting insecurity, Germany experienced those golden years as if there were no barriers, no limitations to finding new ways of self-expression. It was like a grand resurrection of the human spirit from the debris of a frightening past and a terrifying present. Out of a hard and hungry reality arose a need to find oneself, a daring to deny the past. Everyone seemed to be simultaneously at work on something new, in all fields of artistic and humanistic expression.

The whole world is indebted to this rare creative euphoria in Germany and Austria during the 1920's, for the scope of its intellectual growth has had tremendous influence on our lives. The revolutionary ideas of Einstein, Planck and Heisenberg advanced fundamental science with accelerating speed. Psychoanalysis became a household word. Schools of philosophy, ranging from Wittgenstein's positivism to Heidegger's phenomenology and the work of Frankfurt's Institute for Sociological Studies, established mystifying but fascinating relations between society and esthetics.

There was the powerful impact of the enigmatic voice of Franz Kafka. New concepts from the Bauhaus, wedding arts and crafts with technology and the slogan of *Neue Sachlichkeit* (New Objectivity), changed the architectural face of the cities and much of our thinking. Oskar Schlemmer's experimental dance figures stunned people, and later had some tangential influence on Alwin Nikolais's nonobjective dance approach. Expressionism and militant dadaism, flowing into Freudian-inspired surrealism, vied with futurism and constructivism, and all these "isms" flourished in creative competitiveness.

We can draw a wide arc from Thomas Mann and Hermann Hesse to Bertold Brecht and Franz Werfel, from Rilke to Hofmannsthal. A rich and varied palette embraces Arnold Schoenberg and his pupil Alban Berg, Ernst Krenek and Kurt

Weill. The German movie industry reached new heights with Erich von Stroheim and Marlene Dietrich, and with such sophisticated directors as Fritz Lang and Ernst Lubitsch. But the rise of inflation crippled the industry, and it was bought up in its entirety by Paramount and M-G-M.

A new awareness of space led to experimental stage concepts for which the Berlin theatres became famous: ramps, platforms and stairs were used by Max Reinhardt and Leopold Jessner, a treadmill and films by Erwin Piscator's epic theatre. Reinhardt began to stage plays in circus arenas, cathedrals and castles—already at that time creating environmental art. It gave him huge spaces to fill with actors who could no longer stand still and declaim their lines, but who had to move around and let space motivate their acting.

Mary Wigman said of her dancing that space became her dancing partner. Movement consciousness led to a defined and definable space awareness. It began with Rudolf Laban, where it was basic to his visionary concepts. This mystic philosopher had a scientific mind, teaching and preaching the gospel of the magic of movement through which the individual could gain a heightened perception of himself. Laban endeavored to see man grow beyond his average-ness—a Nietzschean thought—and reach for a lofty state of festive existence. This thought inspired the huge pageants he loved to stage.

Kurt Jooss, a young man in the early 1920's, was trying to find his personal road to self-fulfillment in the world of dance. It was self-evident that he should seek the tutoring hand of some brilliant man such as Rudolf Laban. It was as if Jooss was born again when he entered the magic circle of this master over movement. Yet there was another man who also exerted great influence on Kurt Jooss, a literary man who gave him the intellectual stimulation he was seeking.

In 1976 I met Kurt Jooss in his New York hotel on 57th Street. We talked, among other things, about his reading habits. He told me that he had always read much poetry aloud, together with his wife. She brought the poetic world of Stefan George closer to him, while he tried to convince her of Rilke's greatness. Jooss had always had a weakness for first editions and very old books which he collected. But what is most important in the context of this essay is the literary source that he cited as having had the greatest influence on him. He found a strong inspiration for his Weltanschauung (World View) and choreography in the magazine *Die Weltbühne*, edited by Carl von Ossietsky, and particularly in the political writings of its major contributor, Kurt Tucholsky.

Among the many magazines that dominated the newsstands in Germany (and in the bigger cities all over Europe), *Die Weltbühne* was rather inconspicuous. Its circulation hardly ever exceeded 15,000. But strangely enough it had a great intellectual impact: its message was heard, whether despised or praised. It seemed as if everyone read each issue, in spite of its limited printings. Its word counted, among the intellectuals and in the daily political struggle, and in time *Die Weltbühne* achieved a world-wide renown. In such a context it is not surprising that Kurt Jooss's attention was riveted on this magazine and on the key personality among its contributors.

Die Weltbühne was often reproached for saying "No!" to everything, for wallowing in the debunking of both rulers and ruled, for dirtying its own German nest. In the eyes of most of its readers, the name of Kurt Tucholsky was almost synonymous with the ideas of the magazine. He was a major contributor under his own name, and he wrote under four pennames at the same time, often jokingly referring to his "five finger writing." He carried a torch to light up the critical message that the Weimar Republic was on its way to defeat and disaster. German feelings of frustration and humiliation after the war (notwithstanding that it had been unleashed by the Kaiser's Reich in Teutonic arrogance and conducted with methodical brutality) would not be resolved through a corrupt and frivolous game of politics in which the wrong people were kept in power so that everyone on the right could lay claim to being right.

Tucholsky tried to reach the conscience of the German people, to ask for fair play and to fight hypocrisy and greed. "What we need is a sense of decency," he wrote. "Since 1913 I have belonged to those who believe the German spirit to be almost unalterably poisoned ... Are we dirtying our own nests? It is impossible to dirty an Augean stable and it is insane to sit on the fallen roof of an old shed and sing national anthems."

He was often called "corrosive" in his critique of his own country, but as a political phenomenon the Germany of those days was a monstrosity, inherently perpetuating the nationalistic concepts of the vanished Kaiser Reich. The leftists considered the Republic "bourgeois" while for the conservatives it was "Marxist." The moderates feared the radicalisms to the right and to the left, but they feared a socialist revolution more than they feared a Putsch of the radical right. In Tucholsky's words:

We stand before a Germany full of unheard-of corruption, full of profiteers and sneaks, full of three hundred thousand devils, each of whom uses the law in order that his dark person may remain untouched by the revolution. We mean him and only him. And if we have the opportunity to choose, shall we fight him with love, shall we fight him with hate? We want to fight with hate growing out of love ...

One can and probably ought to be a critic of his country and his time without being an enemy of its promise. In his vain attempt to point his five fingers at the ills of the German mind, at his country's social inadequacies and at the lies of its ruling bureaucracy, Tucholsky wanted the people to see the dangers awaiting them—dangers that were to lead to a cataclysm that engulfed the whole world.

It is safe to say that Kurt Jooss saw in Kurt Tucholsky his literary mirror image. Jooss must have felt as Tucholsky did, looking at the Weimar Republic after the revolution of 1918: "We have not had a revolution in Germany, but we've had a counterrevolution." The liberals and socialists found themselves in the awkward position of advocating democracy while fighting the regime that called itself democratic.

When Tucholsky asked himself, in 1919, "What can satire do?" his reply was "Everything!" And he did satirize everything, from the most minor human failings and foibles to the deep immorality in human beings, shown above all in their political crimes. Ten years later, when the rise of Nazism seemed inevitable, Tucholsky lost his belief that one could stem the onslaught of hungry and desperate people caught in a mass psychotic frenzy, that satire could be instrumental in turning the tide of history. Satire was certainly not able to prevent Germany, so proud of its culture, from falling into the inferno of bestial inhumanity.

Tucholsky had fought a valiant battle. But in the years between 1926 and 1932 a spiritual exhaustion gripped him, a feeling of final defeat. He had tried to cleanse the air that the German people were forced to breathe, to halt the descent and to improve a rather hopeless situation. But despair was slowly overwhelming him. On August 7, 1928, he wrote to a friend that he had become desperate about his own writings: "it is very bad because I would like to be silent and remain silent."

Neither Kurt Jooss nor any member of the public knew about this. On the contrary, these were the years when Tucholsky was a celebrity in Germany. His works were newly edited and published. The satires he wrote for the *Vossische Zeitung* brought him fame as a humorist. But he had lost heart for the struggle. Probably Jooss's admiration for Tucholsky rose together with the writer's popularity. The public knows nothing or very little about the inner trials of an artist. Of course, Tucholsky remained for everyone the symbol of integrity, the incessant fighter for decency and human rights with a humorous and often vitriolic pen. His influence on the intelligentsia and the artists remained great.

Erich Kästner said that "Tucholsky wanted to stop a catastrophe with a typewriter." In that context Kurt Jooss wanted to stop the next world war with a satiric ballet called *The Green Table*. Tucholsky became overwhelmed with despair and Kurt Jooss probably with a fighting fury. Did he have to make this balletic statement as a matter of principle or only to ease his conscience, well knowing that the audiences of *The Green Table* would not be able to turn the political tide?

The continued popularity of this ballet on stages all over the world proves the artistic validity of this indisputable classic and of its *cri de coeur* against the dangers that gave birth to the work and from whose grip mankind is not yet delivered.

Choreography and Dance
1993, Vol 3, Part 2, pp. 7-24
Photocopying permitted by license only

Kurt Jooss: the evolution of an artist

Suzanne K. Walther

Kurt Jooss was born shortly after the turn of this century, a time that ushered in the Age of Modernism. His achievement places him in the ranks of those leading artists who have permanently changed our cultural landscape. The significant stages of his career roughly correspond to the major cultural and political events that influenced the lives of his generation. The first and possibly most important period of Jooss's artistic development spanned the years of the Weimar Republic from 1918 to 1932. His career received a major setback when the Nazi regime drove him from Germany in 1933. He escaped to England, where at Dartington Hall he continued his work by organizing a dance community that included his school and his company. Jooss's career took its final turn when in 1949 he accepted the invitation to return to his homeland. His renewed artistic and pedagogical efforts in postwar West Germany led to the eventual development of the postmodern German Tanztheater.

KEY WORDS   "Neue Tanzbühne", Rudolf Laban, Sigurd Leeder, "Ballets Jooss", Dartington Hall, "Folkwangschule".

Kurt Jooss was born on January 12, 1901 in Wasseralfingen in the Baden-Wurttemberg region of Germany near the historic city of Stuttgart. His family owned farm land and his father expected Jooss to inherit and manage the estate. However, Jooss himself was drawn to the arts. Instead of thinking of a career in farm management, his attention was taken up with music, drama and the visual arts. He played the piano and studied singing and drama. Because he felt that he lacked the talent to paint or draw, he took up photography.

His father allowed him to pursue his artistic goals freely. Both of Jooss's parents had artistic talents themselves: his father was an amateur theatre producer and his mother a trained singer. As a teenager Jooss also tried his hand at amateur theatricals. At the age of fourteen he created several movement improvisations, including one entitled *Salome* and another *Indian Prayer*. Instinctively Jooss searched for a medium of expression that would consolidate his talents and give him personal satisfaction.

At the age of eighteen, after graduating from the *Realgymnasium* of Aalen, Jooss entered the Stuttgart Academy of Music. In spite of being a success at his studies, especially in acting and voice, he was dissatisfied. In an autobiographical essay he wrote:

I studied drama devotedly and with great success but I remained empty. Something was missing everywhere, and I no longer believed in my dream of the arts. (Markard, 1985, p. 29)

He was on the verge of giving up his quest for a suitable artistic expression and

Figure 1   Kurt Jooss—Self Portrait, approx. 1918 (Jooss Archives).

nearly resigned himself to a life of agricultural management when by chance he met Rudolf von Laban.[1] He had been taking lessons in movement from Grete Heid, a former Laban pupil. It was through her that the two men met: a meeting that changed the course of Jooss's life and to some extent the course of dance history.

During the years 1920 to 1922, Laban lived and taught in Stuttgart and served as Ballet Master at the Mannheim Opera. Shortly after Jooss became his student, Laban included him in a group of twenty-five dancers whom he trained for professional performances. They appeared at the Mannheim Opera together with the Opera Ballet in Laban's own works. Jooss instantly became one of the leading dancers of this group. As Jooss modestly remembers:

Figure 2   Kurt Jooss—"Training in Ascona 1925" (Jooss Archives).

A few weeks later I danced the male lead in our first work, *Die Geblendeten* [*The Deluded*], with great success. At that time in Germany one did not need great proficiency for the "Expressionist Dance": strong intensity was all-convincing. In the meantime though I have added to my abilities. (Markard & Markard, p. 18)[2]

Laban straight away recognized Jooss's exceptional ability and made him his assistant and later regisseur of his company, the *Tanzbühne Laban*. Jooss served as one of Laban's model dancers who was able to physically execute and demonstrate Laban's movement experiments (Coton, 1946, p. 16). He also participated in the summer training camps in Ascona, Switzerland. Laban called it his "dance farm;" his pupils lived in a commune, close to nature, and practised a form of minimal subsistence farming (Laban, 1875, pp. 85–86). It was there, in practices held in the open air, that Jooss first participated in Laban's monumental choric works. These and other works were performed during the *Tanzbühne Laban*'s residencies in Stuttgart, Mannheim and Hamburg, and during its tours all over Germany.

While Jooss was a member of Laban's group, two important people entered his life. One was his future wife, the other a lifelong friend: both became his artistic collaborators.

In 1921, a year after Jooss's arrival, a new pupil entered the group. She had the exotic foreign name of Aino Siimola. She had been born in 1901 in the town of Narva, in Russian Estonia. This town was located inland from the Gulf of Finland, not far from the historic city of St. Petersburg. Siimola was educated in a private school that was directed by Maria Fedorovna, mother of the Russian Tzarina. Dance was one of the requirements of the curriculum.

Having chosen to become a professional dancer, Siimola decided to travel to Germany with the purpose of studying with Laban. After a short apprenticeship in Stuttgart, she became a member of the *Tanzbühne Laban*. She was a woman of great beauty and intelligence, and after she became Jooss's wife she also became his lifelong artistic collaborator.

While working with Laban in Hamburg in 1924, Jooss met a young native of that Northern city named Sigurd Leeder. Leeder studied art at the Hamburg School of Arts and Crafts. He also studied acting and took movement classes from a former student of Laban. His skills and education complemented Jooss's, and so did his looks and his temperament.

Jooss had a strong personality: he was brimming with curiosity and overflowing with abundant creative energy. Leeder was frail and finely chiselled, with a sense for form, detail and craftsmanship. The two artists complemented each other in temperament.

Jooss began choreographing early in his career, while he was still working with Laban. He created a program of short dances or *Kammertänze*, "chamber dances". Shortly after they met, Jooss and Leeder put together a program called *Two Male Dancers*. The concept of a male duo of concert dancers appearing without props or a supporting cast was new and original. The choreography was experimental, influenced greatly by Laban's theories and movement studies (Coton, 1946, p. 16). The program was exceptionally well balanced, consisting of four duets and four solos for each dancer. It filled an entire evening's time. The subjects ranged from religious themes to comical parodies reflecting upon the times. It included ethnic dance and Jazz which was still quite new in Europe, having just recently crossed the Atlantic. Only a few photographs remain of these dances, but Jooss stands out in them for his comic talent and character sketches.

In 1924 Niedecken-Gebhardt invited Jooss to join him at the Municipal Theatre of Münster as "movement regisseur" and ballet master. Niedecken-Gebhardt's novel approach to opera staging included the conviction that movement should be an integral part of the production. He needed a movement specialist to accomplish this goal. Jooss, who was ready to strike out on his own, accepted the position. Jooss had achieved recognition as a choreographer and performer in his own right, with a distinctive style and original point of view. He wrote:

I needed independence for my further development, so, with regret, I left the " Tanzbühne Laban". (Markard & Markard, 1985, p. 35)

Jooss then took the opportunity to establish his own company, *Die Neue Tanzbühne*. When Laban's performing group ran into financial difficulties on a Yugoslavian tour and had to disband, Jooss offered positions in his company to a few of the Laban dancers. His group was small, initially consisting of three male and four female dancers (Markard, 1982, p. 18).

Die Neue Tanzbühne was technically a part of the Municipal Theatre of Münster, but it was artistically independent. It was entirely under the artistic direction of Jooss. In his productions he made use of the many talented people working in the Münster Theatre. Hein Heckroth created the designs for seven of the eight ballets Jooss choreographed during this period. His work contributed greatly to the unity of concept in these productions.

It was also during this time that the composer F.A. Cohen became Jooss's musical collaborator. Cohen had definite ideas about creating music for dance. He believed that the musical accompaniment should underlie the dramatic meaning of the dance, accentuate the choreographic form and rhythmically aid the dancer. Jooss and Cohen shared the belief that choreography and musical composition should proceed together to give expression of the dramatic idea in unified style and form. The greatest surviving example of this collaboration is *The Green Table*. In the next few years the Municipal Theatre of Münster achieved fame for its innovative productions under Niedecken-Gebhardt and the opera director Rudolf Schultz-Dornburg, and Jooss's group also became widely known in Germany.

Performances were mainly held in the Münster Theatre, but the *Neue Tanzbühne* also toured throughout the country, stopping at such major cities as Berlin, Bonn, Hamburg, and Mannheim. The eight pieces Jooss choreographed during this two year period included shorter works such as *Larven* (1925), *Der Dämon* (1925), *Groteske* (1925) and *Kaschemme* (1926). Of *Groteske* he wrote:

a tiny piece which, however, showed clearly in which direction my work was to develop: away from the literal, aspiring toward a physically and spiritually motivated dance movement and art form. (Markard, 1982, p. 19)

Der Dämon was choreographed to music by Hindemith and it is described as "an expressionistic ballet with symbolic figures" (Hager, p. 2). The word *larve* means both larva and mask in German, a double meaning which gave special poignancy to this group work. A string of crouching figures in hooded masks and capes presented mixed images of the nature of bugs and people, or the "human insect."

The two longer pieces were entitled *Die Brautfahrt* (1925) and *Tragödie* (1926). The libretti for both were created by Jooss. *Die Brautfahrt* was a fairy tale in four acts, later renamed by Jooss *A Spring Tale* (1939). In this dance Jooss once again made observations on human behavior. Jooss considered *Tragödie* his most important work of this period, not only because of its complexity but also because its creation was motivated by his own personal trauma of breaking away from his mentor Rudolf Laban. It was a full length ballet in four acts for four soloists and a chorus, to music improvised by F.A. Cohen for each performance.

Meanwhile Jooss had been deeply concerned with the state of dance education in Germany. He believed that German modern dance lacked the kind of systematic dance training which gave classical dancers a highly developed technique. In the spring of 1925, he and Leeder worked out a plan for a professional dance school. He wrote:

We saw the greatest need for the New Dance to be a firmly consolidated system of teaching, and we decided to abandon all other wishes and work solely to this purpose. Laban's movement teachings and choreographic space principles, combined with the discipline of traditional ballet, were to make up our materials. (Markard, 1982, p. 19)

In the fall of 1925, a group of artists including Jooss and Leeder established a new school which was named the *Westfälischen Akademie Für Bewegung, Sprache und Music* (Westphalian Academy of Movement, Speech and Music). The school was under the overall direction of Rudolf Schulz-Dornburg, who was also the music director of the Münster Theatre. Jooss was the Director of the dance division, Vilma Monckeberg headed the division of speech, and Hermann Erpf was in charge of the music division (Markard & Markard, 1985, p. 145). The school developed rapidly, and two years later it moved to Essen to be incorporated into the newly-founded *Folkwangschule*.

Leeder had decided to dedicate himself to dance education. He had a genuine interest in teaching, and concerns about his health also contributed to his decision to change the direction of his career. He had medical problems with his lungs. Because he seemed better during the summer vacations when he spent much time outdoors, his doctors recommended that he not return full time to the unhealthy, dusty air of the stage and rehearsal hall. From then on he concentrated on dance pedagogy and became one of the most significant European modern dance teachers. He was the greatest exponent of the Jooss-Leeder technique of dance. His positions included that of chief instructor at the Folkwangschule (1927–1934), co-director of the Jooss-Leeder School in England (1934–1940) and ballet master of the Ballets Jooss (1942–1947).

In order to enlarge the scope of their knowledge of dance, Jooss and Leeder decided to study abroad. So far Jooss had only mastered modern dance and he felt it necessary to acquire a first-hand knowledge of classical ballet. In December 1926 the two of them went to Paris to take class with the émigrée Russian ballerina Lubov Egorova. She was a graduate of the Imperial Ballet School and a principal dancer with the Maryinsky Theatre, now the Kirov Ballet. She exemplified the unsurpassed tradition of a school and the purity and artistry of a technique, the representatives of which like royalty form a lineage to the present day.

In a short period of time Jooss acquired an understanding of classical ballet that convinced him of its value, importance and historical significance. He never stopped defending his view, unique at the time, that ballet and modern dance are not opposing techniques but belong on a historical continuum in the realm of dance. He believed that all available means should be used for the expression of significant human emotion. He made this clear in a statement at the International Congress of the Dance in Paris in June 1932:

We aim therefore at discovering a choreography deriving equally from the contributions of modern art and from the classic Ballet. We find the basis of our work in the whole range of human feeling and all phases of its infinite expression; and by concentration on the "Essential" we arrive at our form in the Dance.[3]

The combined use of ballet and modern dance techniques in choreography was a completely novel position at the time. Modern dance was proclaimng its revolt against the academic restraints of ballet, and the various exponents of *Ausdruckstanz* feuded amongst themselves, each proclaiming to hold a superior point of view.

In 1926, as an addition to the program of *Two Male Dancers*, a masked dance was planned by Jooss and Leeder, tentatively called *Dance of Death*. Jooss described the plan as follows:

We intended to work with masks, which would enable us to quickly slip into different characters (beggar, peasant woman, bishop, king, courtesan), since we were only two people. (Markard, 1982, p. 18).

As a trained artist, Leeder was proficient in the design and execution of masks. He created eight sculptural likenesses of the human face, each mask with a different expression. Each depicted a particular character, who in the course of the dance would die according to the way he had lived (Coton, 1946, p. 88). This was the small seed of a much greater concept that six years later came to fruition in Jooss's masterpiece, *The Green Table*.

Because of an unfortunate accident, the *Dance of Death* was never added to the program of concert dances. In January 1927 Jooss and Leeder were rehearsing in Vienna under the direction of the acclaimed theatre director Dr. Hans Niedecken-Gebhart for a performance. Gertrude Boden-weiser's local school supplied the movement choir and Jooss and Leeder were to dance solos choreographed by Jooss in a scenic oratorio of Händel's *Herakles*. During one of the rehearsals Jooss leaped off a tall pedestal and wrenched his knee in landing. The performance of *Herakles*, as well as a "Two Male Dancers" performance in Vienna had to be cancelled.

Within a month he was completely disabled, and spent ten weeks off his feet recuperating from severe knee joint injury. The arthritis in his knee caused by this incident kept him in discomfort for the rest of his life.[4] Jooss remembered, with a note of dismay:

That was the end of our touring plans and as I thought also the end of my performing career. Buried was the tour of "Two Male Dancers", buried the "Dance of Death" for which there were no performers. (Markard & Markard, 1985, p. 33)

Meanwhile the Municipal Theatre of Münster decided under public pressure that its artistic direction was too avant-garde. To ease the minds of the conservative municipal authorities, changes in programs and personnel were instituted. Among the people leaving were Niedecken-Gebhardt, Schulz-Dornburg, Cohen (for personal reasons)[5] and the entire *Neue Tanzbühne*, which at this time was under the direction of one of its members, Jens Keith. In early 1927 Jooss was concentrating all his efforts on a new pedagogical endeavor.

Fortunately for the *Neue Tanzbühne*, Schulz-Dornburg obtained the position of music director at the Essen Opera House and invited the entire company to join him there for the 1927–1928 season, with Keith as ballet master. In June 1927 the dance group performed two Jooss ballets, *Kaschemme* and *Groteske*, at the First German Dancer's Congress at Magdeburg.

In the spring of 1927, while Jooss was in Münster recuperating from his knee injury, he began negotiations with the mayor of Essen, who wanted Jooss to direct the dance division at a new school for the visual and the performing arts. Jooss accepted the position. Together with Rudolf Schulz-Dornburg and Max Fielder he moved his *Westfälishe Schule* to Essen, which became the core· for the founding of the Folkwangschule (Markard & Markard, 1985, p. 145).

In the early 1920's the city of Essen had acquired a sizable art collection named *Folkwang*.[6] In 1927 it was decided to sponsor a school of the performing arts. It was conceived as a sister school to the existing school of design, arts and crafts. The city wanted all three of its cultural institutions, the museum and the two schools, to carry the mythological name *Folkwang*. Thus, when Jooss's school was brought to Essen it became the *Folkwang Schule für Tanz, Musik und Sprechen*.

Meanwhile Jooss's knee did not get better. Hoping for a cure, he travelled to a

Figure 3 The "New Team" for Essen: Hein Heckrot, Kurt Jooss, F.A. Cohen (Jooss Archives).

small Hungarian town named Pistyan (consequently Piest'any in Slovakian as a part of Czechoslovakia) known for its medicinal hot springs. He stayed for six weeks at the spa, and while his knee was being treated with mud baths he spent the time working on dance notation. He started with the idea that movement sequences should be recorded on a vertical staff, where the right side represented the right side of the human body and the left the corresponding left side. Next he added the idea that the weight-bearing support of the body (the legs) should be represented on the middle shaft, while the arms and the head should be located on shafts further out. Jooss called this the *Linien System* (Linear System) of notation.

In the summer of 1927 Jooss and Leeder continued to work on the notation system and completed the notation of two solos, the *Courting Dance of the Princes* (*Werbetanz des Prinzen*) from Jooss's ballet *Die Brautfahrt,* and Leeder's *Maskentanz.* They attended a summer course of Laban's where they studied *Eukinetics* with Dussia Bereska, and took the occasion to present their developments for the notation system to Laban. Laban took up their scheme with enthusiasm and elaborated it extensively with the assistance of his disciples. This became the notation system known as Labanotation in English and as Kinetographie Laban in German. Laban acknowledged Jooss's contribution to his notation system in a preface to one of his books:

I will mention here Kurt Jooss, who, after finishing his studies as a pupil of Bereska and myself, surprised us one day with a proposal to duplicate Feuillet's right-left division of the movement sequences. We proceeded then to record the movements of trunk and arms in separate columns instead of inserting them in the upper part of the cross mentioned beforehand.[7] (Laban, 1976, p. x)

In 1928, at the Second German Dancers Congress in Essen, Laban officially presented his notation system to the public. Critic A.V. Coton writes:

Laban's personal efforts were eagerly taken up in his circle of disciples and collaborators, and the "Kinetographie Laban" as first published at the Dance Congress at Essen in 1928 was the result of this joint effort of which the main exponents were, besides Laban himself, Kurt Jooss, Sigurd Leeder, Albrecht Knust and Dussia Bereska. (1946, p. 80)

The Congress, which was organized by Jooss, ran from June 21st to 26th. In his opening statement Jooss addressed the issue of the relationship of classical ballet to modern dance. He maintained that it was important not to lose sight of the achievements of the classical tradition, and to consider how this tradition and technique might contribute to the evolution of German modern dance. He was a lone crusader in this advocacy of combining classical and modern dance techniques. "I was nearly stoned for that," he said later, referring to the reactions of the participants to his speech (quoted in Häger, in press).

Ultimately Jooss proved his point through his own choreography. It is fair to say that no choreographer in the history of dance has combined the classical and modern techniques in the service of theatrical dance drama as successfully as Jooss.

For Jooss, technique was a means for expression, choreography the form of content. By 1927, when he co-founded the Folkwangschule in Essen, he was a mature artist with a repertory of eight group works, at least four major solos, several duets and numerous dances staged and performed for operas and operettas. He had founded a school and developed a method of dance training. He was deeply committed to the theatre, to professional training for dancers, and to collaborative work with other art professionals. As Häger points out, at this time:

Laban was the dominating pace setter, Wigman the leading artist, but from the time of the Congress Jooss began to emerge as a new spiritual leader [of the dance world]. (Häger, in press)

The theme of the Second Dancers Congress at Essen was the relationship of modern dance to the traditional theatre. There were differing points of view. Some, Like Max Terpis, student of Wigman and ballet master of the Berlin State Opera, held that the *Podiumstänzer* (recital or concert dancer) should not exist within the traditional boundaries of the theatre. Wigman envisioned an utopian performing space based on the needs of movement artists. Laban together with Jooss advocated the professional theatre as the place for dance as a performing art. Among this group was Yvonne Georgi, who said:

Those who create dances for the theatre must have the ability, not only to involve themselves and their own feelings in the dance, but to arrive at a *Gesamtkunstwerk* [complete work of art] by giving form and shape to their surroundings (stage-space, costumes, lighting, decor, movement) and their own expression. (Koegler, 1974, p. 11)

We hear the echo of the word *Gesamtkunstwerk* from as far back in German art history as Richard Wagner. The Bauhaus was the institutionalized embodiment of the concept of "total design" in the visual arts. Jooss might have been influenced by the concept when he worked on developing the dance curriculum at the Folkwangschule.

The municipality of Essen gave the following description of the school in announcing its opening:

On Oct. 1 the City of Essen will open the Folkwang Schools, two divisions offering education in all fields of the Arts. The "School of Arts and Crafts" (*Kunstgewerbeschule*) will receive a new subtitle, "School of Form." The "School for Expressive Arts" (*Schule für Ausdruckskunst*) is conceived as a school for music, dance and speech, also including theathre, art history and criticism. (Quoted in Markard & Markard, 1985, p. 145)

In 1928 Jooss formed a small performing group of professional dancers and called it the Folkwang Tanztheater Studio. F.A. Cohen joined him as a composer, pianist and music teacher. When Jooss assumed the post of Ballet Director at the Essen Opera in 1929, he consolidated his studio group with the Opera dancers and gave it the name *Folkwang Tanzbühne Essen*. Of the sixteen major ballets Jooss choreographed for these groups, only four survive. They consistitute his entire choreographic legacy.[8]

But Jooss's legacy includes more than his choreography. It includes an aesthetic and pedagogical method that is alive (though metamorphosed) in today's German *Tanztheater* and in the continued functioning of the Folkwangschule. Jooss outlined his theories on dance education in a memorandum he wrote in 1927 for the establishment of a German Dance Academy. Later he expanded this into a detailed proposal for a complete professional program for the choreographing, performing, directing, notating, and teaching of dance. He wrote:

The teaching method of the school combines "classical ballet" and "modern dance" as complementary factors in a new synthesis. Both technique and artistic usage are revealed to the student by the use of *contrasting* characteristics of both these disciplines and the possibility of their harmonious synthesis. (Markard & Markard, 1985, p. 151)

To the critics who accused him of not teaching a specific "Jooss technique", Jooss had the following to say:

I am often reproached that the style we teach is not clearly identifiable. But we are not teaching a specific style; what we teach is the dancer's craft. Style is a result of choreographic intention and choice. (Markard & Markard, 1985, p. 149)

The *Folkwang Tanzbühne* was the resident company of the Essen Opera house. It gained world recognition at the *Grand Concours International de Choregraphie* in Paris on July 3, 1932, when it performed *The Green Table*, the sensational winner of the first prize. During the fall of 1932 the company became a separate organization under the new name of *Ballets Jooss* and began an extensive touring program. But the company was destined never to return from the foreign tour that it undertook in 1933: like so much else, it became a casuality of Hitler.

Jooss belonged to the generation of artists who matured between the two World Wars. He was a creative participant in the Weimar culture, and like many of his contemporaries he developed a strong social conscience. He had seen the ravages of the war and felt emotionally close to the works of Otto Dix, George Grosz and Bertolt Brecht, each of whom was concerned with the resulting social and political ills. He read the works of Kurt Tucholksky who was openly critical of the widespread right-wing militarism. His own work reflected the artistic trend known as *Die Neue Sachlichkeit* or New Objectivity. As its name suggests, the focus of the movement was to observe and depict everyday life, objectively presented. Humor, irony, caricature and real drama were characteristic of the movement, and Jooss used them all. Most of all, he was conscious of creating artistic forms that not only expressed but were a direct consequence of their content:

We are living in an age which is rediscovering *artistic form*. In dance this means that out of the chaos of arbitrary and haphazard movements only the essentially important will be developed, with an economy and restriction appropriate to art, and in the purest possible form. (Quoted in Markard & Markard, 1985, p. 17)

In 1933 Jooss was forced to flee Nazi Germany. That year a German newspaper published an article with this lengthy title: "The Truthful Jacob, KURT JOOSS AS MOSES' TEMPLE DANCER: Without Cohen the Jew he Cannot Fulfill his Artistic Mission." Jooss personally went to the headquarters of the Nazi Party to protest their demand that he dismiss the Jewish members of his company (Markard & Markard, 1985, p. 51). His uncompromising attitude led the Nazis to escalate their rhetoric, and the *Ballets Jooss* was accused of harboring not only Jews, but also Kultur-Bolsheviks and homosexuals. Jooss had exposed himself to great danger, and was warned by the Freemasons that his arrest was imminent. An escape was arranged and Jooss fled to Holland with the entire company. These events brought to a sudden end the first and probably the most creative phase of Jooss's career.

After the flight from Nazi Germany, while the Ballets Jooss was on tour through Europe and America, Jooss received an invitation from a wealthy British couple, Leonard and Dorothy Elmhirst, to bring his school to England (Markard & Markard, 1985, p. 55). Thus began a new chapter in Jooss's life and career. In April of 1934 his school re-opened at Dartington Hall in Devon, England, under the name of the "Jooss-Leeder School of Dance." Sigurd Leeder left the Folkwangschule of Essen for Dartington Hall with the teaching staff and twenty-three students that formed the initial core of the school.

For more than a year the Ballets Jooss was without a permanent home. Nevertheless Jooss kept on creating important new works for them. His second version of *The Prodigal Son* dates from this period, as does a light humorous piece to Purcell's music entitled *The Seven Heroes*. The story of the ballet was based on a Grimm fairy tale set in a idyllic rural community (Coton, 1946, p. 56).

Jooss left the company for a while to accept an invitation by the exotic ballerina Ida Rubinstein to choreograph and direct the world premiere of Stravinsky's *Persephone* for the Paris Opera. For a brief time the company had to disband for lack of financial support. Finally, in September 1935, exactly two years after Jooss's departure from Germany, the Ballets Jooss was re-established at Dartington Hall (Markard & Markard, 1985, p. 55). A core group of dancers from the original company were joined by pupils of the school. Jooss added three new ballets to the repertory: *Ballade, Johann Strauss Tonight*, and *The Mirror*. The entire new program was produced that year in the newly built Barn Theatre at Dartington Hall.

The Mirror was a sequel to *The Green Table*. This ballet was also a collaboration between Jooss, F.A. Cohen and Hein Heckroth. Both works dealt with the impact of war. In *The Green Table* the focus is on the figure of Death and his victims, while in *The Mirror* Jooss shows us the survivors. The work "reflects the confusion and worries, the despair and the hopes of post-war mankind struggling to escape from the moral, social and political consequences of his own folly" (Coton, 1946, p. 59). The scenario focused on the grim realities of postwar civilian existence.

Much later, after his return to Germany, Jooss choreographed a third ballet on the war theme entitled *Journey in the Fog*. This work was influenced by his own experiences during the Second World War. It consisted of four scenes, each one reflecting on a different aspect of hardship and suffering: "the loneliness of exile; the claustrophobia of internment in camp; the shadow of bereavement; and the restlessness of attempted rehabilitation" (Häger, in press). These three works, *Table*, *Mirror* and *Fog*, form a trilogy focussed on the gravest events of our twentieth century, the century shaped by global warfare.

In 1939 Jooss choreographed *Chronica*, a full length ballet dealing with another timely topic: the horrors of dictatorship. His portrayal of a medieval despot and the suffering he inflicts on his subjects made allegorical reference to Hitler and Germany. With the entire new repertory, the Ballets Jooss travelled to the United States in 1940 for an extensive tour, including a long engagement in New York City. Jooss stayed in England, expecting to devote his time to the Jooss-Leeder School of Dance. However, England adopted the wartime policy of evacuating aliens from the coastal areas of England, and the school had to close down. Teachers and students alike were obliged to leave.

Jooss, as a German national, was interned as an "enemy alien" (Markard & Markard, 1985, p. 59). This was a devastating experience for him, although he kept his spirits high. His fellow inmate Robert Ziller is quoted as saying:

In camp he [Jooss] was wonderful. His courage and his patience inspired us all. He never ceased to tell us that England couldn't help herself, and that we who are her friends must understand that and be patient. But in his heart he is very unhappy. (Markard & Markard, 1985, p. 61)

He was freed after six months, following the intervention of some prominent intellectuals. His devoted wife Aino Siimola worked relentlessly for his release.

In 1942 the Ballets Jooss was disbanded once again. Jooss himself was unable to leave England and could not look after his company. The final performances were in New York City, following an extended tour of the United States and Latin America. Ernst Uthoff, his wife Lola Botka, and Rudolph Pescht went to Santiago Chile to form their own ballet company. Some company members got jobs in theatres in New York, and others were offered one-way passage on convoys traveling from the United States to England. This was arranged as a favor to Jooss by the British government, following Jooss's successful staging of Mozart's *Magic Flute* and *Marriage of Figaro* for the Sadler's Wells Opera Company.

The *Ballets Jooss* was re-established for the third time in Cambridge in 1942. Again Jooss added new works to the company's repertory: *Company at the Manor*, to Beethoven's "Spring Sonata", and *Pandora*. Häger describes the latter work as "deeply disturbing." He writes:

Refraining from his customary clarity of message, he created visions of future dangers for humanity, warning against unrestrained curiosity and ingenuity. It was as if he had a presentiment of the atom bomb a year before it happened, and of the evils to follow in its wake. (Häger, in press)

The new repertory of Ballets Jooss premiered at The Haymarket in London two days before D-Day in June 1944. From 1942 on there was a shortage of male dancers so Jooss began performing again. Once again the company left on an international tour.

In 1947 Jooss was finally granted British citizenship. Also in that year, despite government support and popular success, the Ballets Jooss disbanded for the final time. Post-war conditions made it too difficult to continue performing. Jooss embarked on a journey to Chile at the invitation of the Uthoffs. He choreographed *Juventud* for their company, the Chilean National Ballet. He also gave his farewell performance in his greatest role, the part of Death in *The Green Table*. With this another chapter of Jooss's career came to an end.

The final phase of his career began with an invitation from the Folkwangschule in Essen to return as Director of the dance division once again. He was also offered a subsidy from the municipality of Essen for a new dance company. He accepted, and in 1949, with great hopes for the future, he returned to Germany for good. For the next two years he worked at re-establishing the dance program at the Folkwangschule. A leading soloist and teacher at the school, Hans Züllig became his assistant and shared many of the responsibilities. Once again Jooss founded a company, naming it the *Folkwang-Tanztheater der Stadt Essen*. By 1951 the new company went on a West German and European tour. Included in the repertory were restagings of the original Ballets Jooss program. This was the first time that postwar Germany experienced *The Green Table*. Also included on the program were two ballets by Züllig (*La Bosquet* and *Fantasie*) and four new ballets by Jooss: *Columbinade, Dithyrambus, Journey in the Fog,* and *Night Train*. Keeping life in proper perspective in *Night Train* Jooss created a humorous piece about people's dreams during an overnight train journey.

Unfortunately the Folkwang-Tanztheater was short-lived. The municipality of Essen reneged on its promise and refused to extend its financial support. The final curtain came down on the company in 1953. The following comment appeared in a Dutch newspaper, the *Algemeen Hendelsblad*: "It would be tragic and absolutely irresponsible if the most famous German dance group should now be obliged to end its successful activity" (Quoted in Markard & Markard, 1985, p. 69). Jooss's disappointment was especially keen because he believed that the company was on the verge of becoming self-supporting.

Meanwhile Jooss continued his mission as an educator, working at the Folkwangschule and teaching in summer schools in Switzerland. From 1954 to 1956 he directed the Düsseldorf Opera with the hope of establishing a *Tanztheater* there. The administration promised him to help found an independent dance company. When they broke their promise he left. In the next few years he travelled in Europe teaching and choreographing. He established a post graduate Master's Program for Dance under the name of *Folkwang Dance Studio*. The members of these classes were given opportunities to choreograph and to perform. From these Master Classes evolved Jooss's last company, the *Folkwangballet*. In addition to Jooss's choreography, the repertory included works by other distinguished artists such as Antony Tudor's *Jardin Aux Lilas*, Jean Cébron's *Struktur*, and Lucas Hoving's *Songs of Encounter* and *Icarus*. Pina Bausch tried her wings as a choreographer and her first effort *Fragment* was included in the program.

Jooss retired from his post at the Folkwangschule in 1968. He continued to

Figure 4 Kurt Jooss and Pina Bausch in rehearsal for *The Green Table*, Folkwangschule 161–1962 (Photograph van Leewen. Jooss Archives).

work as a guest choreographer, and re-staged his ballets for several companies and art festivals. In 1972 he delegated the responsibility for restaging the original Ballets Jooss program to his daughter, Anna Markard. To this day Miss Markard continues to set these ballets, most importantly *The Green Table*, for dance companies all over the world.

Jooss lost his wife Siimola in 1971. It was a great blow to him, for she had been his lifetime companion and his most trusted artistic adviser. He moved from Essen to Kreuth in Bavaria, where he spent the rest of his life. During the 1970's Jooss was often asked to serve as guest choreographer, but he usually refused. He did accept an invitation to the Salzburg Festival to choreograph Cavalieri's *Rappresentatione di anima e di corpo*, which he considered his last significant work.

Figure 5 Kurt Jooss 1976 in Santa Barbara, USA (Photograph Bergsohn. Jooss Archives).

Jooss died in 1979 in Heilbronn, from injuries sustained in an automobile accident.

In 1976, in celebration of Jooss's seventy-fifth birthday, Robert Joffrey revived the original Ballets Jooss program at the City Center 55th Street Theater. These four ballets—*Big City*, *Pavane on the Death of an Infanta*, *A Ball in Old Vienna*, and *The Green Table*—are all that remain of the forty to fifty ballets Jooss choreographed in his lifetime. Appropriately, their survival owes much to Labanotation, which in turn owes so much to Jooss. But Jooss's artistic legacy goes far beyond those four ballets. He pioneered an approach to dance expression in which content determines form and technique is the direct outcome of dramatic necessity. He was thus a founder of the newest movement in theatrical dance, the German *Tanztheater*.

Notes

1. Laban dropped the "von" from his name in the 1940's and referred to himself from then on plainly as Rudolf Laban.
2. Laban himself alternately refers to this work as a "play" and as "pure dance", suggesting that Jooss's dramatic abilities made up for his lack of technical proficiency.
3. Manuscript in the Elsa Kahl Cohen archives. Elsa Kahl Cohen was a founding member of the Ballets Jooss, and is the widow of the composer F.A. Cohen.
4. Personal notes of Elsa Kahl Cohen, in the author's possession.
5. As the oldest son, F.A. Cohen had taken over the running of the family publishing house after his father died.
6. In Teutonic mythology *Folkwang* was the banquet hall of the goddess of love and beauty Freya. It was located in a great meadow in the sky where heroes were invited to be her guests. The owner of the paintings who donated them for the establishment of the Essen museum chose the name because he intended the museum to be a place where people met to be inspired by creativity.
7. This system of notation was published first in 1928, during Laban's lifetime.
8. The four works are *Pavane on the Death of an Infanta* (1929), *The Green Table* (1932), *Big City* (1932), and *A Ball in Old Vienna* (1932).

Selected Bibliography

Coton, A.V. *The New Ballet: Kurt Jooss and his work*. London: Dennis Dobson, 1946.

De Moroda D. A day with Kurt Jooss. *The Dancing Times*, May 1935, pp. 140-142.

Gay, P. *Weimar culture: the outsider as insider*. Middlesex, England: Penguin Books, 1974. (Originally published, 1969).

Gowing, L. Notes on the Ballets Jooss. *The Dancing Times*, November 1936.

Gropius, W. (Ed.) *The theater of the Bauhaus*. Middletown, Connecticut: Wesleyan University Press, 1961.

Grosz, G. *An autobiography* (rev. ed., N. Hodges, trans.). New York: Macmillan, 1983. (Originally published, 1946.)

———. *Ecce Homo*. New York: Dover Publications, 1971. (Originally published, 1923.)

Gruen, J. *Interview with Kurt Jooss*. Phonotape, 2 cassettes, August 3, 1976. Dance Collection of The New York Public Library at Lincoln Center.

———. *The private world of ballet*. New York: Penguin Books, 1976.

Häger, B. Biography of Kurt Jooss. In *International Encyclopedia of Dance* (S.J. Cohen, Ed.). New York: Macmillan, in press.

Hall, F. An interview with Jooss. *The Dancing Times*, November 1936.

Heidegger, M. *German Existentialism* (D.D. Runes, Ed. and trans.). New York: Philosophical Library, 1967.

Hodgon, J. & Preston-Dunlop, V. *Rudolf Laban: an introduction to his work & influence*. Plymouth: Northcote House, 1990.

Howe, D.S. *Manifestations of the German Expressionist aesthetic as presented in drama and art in the dance and writings of Mary Wigman*. Unpublished doctoral dissertation, University of Wisconsin-Madison, 1985. UMI 8512305

Hutchinson, A. *The Big City in Labanotation*. Microfilm. The New York Public Library, 1955.

———. *The Green Table in Labanotation*. Notated in 1939. Microfilm. The New York Public Library, 1955.

———. *Labanotation*. New York: Theatre Arts Books, 1977.

———. *Pavane in Labanotation*. Notated in 1938. Microfilm. The New York Public Library, 1954.

Huxley, M. The Green Table, a dance of death: Kurt Jooss in an interview with Michael Huxley. *Ballet International*, August-September 1982, pp. 8-12.

Hynninem, A. *Labanotation score of Big City*. Notated in 1974. New York: Dance Notation Bureau.

Jooss, K. *Choreographische Harmonielehre*. Neue Music-Zeitung (Stuttgart), 1928, 49(7).

———. The dance of the future (an interview with Derra de Moroda). *The Dancing Times*, August 1933, pp. 453-455.

———. Rudolf von Laban on his 60th birthday. *The Dancing Times*, December 1939, pp. 129-131.

Kendall, E. *Where she danced*. New York: Alfred A. Knopf, 1979.

Kessler, H. *In the twenties* (C. Kessler, trans.). New York: Holt, Reinhart and Winston, 1971.

Kirstein, L. *Dance: a short history of theatrical dancing*. New York: Dance Horizons, 1977. (Originally published, 1935.)

Kisselgoff, A. How much does dance owe to Jooss? *The New York Times*, July 11, 1982, section 2, p. 17.

——. That German accent in American modern dance. *The New York Times*, February 5, 1989, section 2, p. 24.

Koch, R. I'm a playwright of movement. *The New York Times*, March 14, 1988, section 2, p. 8.

Koegler, H. In the shadow of the swastica; dance in Germany, 1927-1936. *Dance Perspectives 57*, 1974.

Laban, R. *A life for dance* (L. Ullmann, trans.). London: Macdonald & Evans, 1975. (Originally published, 1935.)

——, *Choreutics* (L. Ullmann, Ed and trans.). Boston: Plays Inc., 1974. (Originally published, 1966.)

——, *The language of movement: a guidebook to choreutics* (L. Ullmann, Ed. and trans.). Boston: Plays Inc., 1974. (Originally published, 1966.)

——. *The mastery of movement* (L. Ullmann, Ed. and trans.). Boston: Plays Inc., 1975. (Originally published, 1950.)

Lange, R. (Ed.) *Laban's principles of dance and movement notation* (2nd ed.). Boston: Plays Inc., 1975. (Originally published, 1956.)

Laqueur, W. *Weimar: a cultural history 1918-1933*. New York: Perigee Books, 1980. (Originally published 1974.)

Langer, R. The post-war German Expressionism of Pina Bausch and her Wuppertal Dance Theater (R. Sikes, trans.). *Dance Magazine*, June 1984, pp. 46–53.

Leeder, S. Rudolf Laban, an appreciation. *The Dancing Times*, August 1958, p. 511.

Levinson, A. The modern dance in Germany. *Theater Arts*, February 1929, pp. 143–153.

Maletic, V. *Body space expression: the development of Rudolf Laban's movement and dance concepts*. New York: Mouton de Gruyer, 1987.

——. Wigman and Laban: the interplay of theory and practice. *Ballet Review*, 1986, 14(3), 86–95.

Manning, S.A. An American perspective on Tanztheater. *The Drama Review*, 1986, 110, pp. 67–79.

——. *Body politic: the dances of Mary Wigman*. Unpublished doctoral dissertation, Columbia University, 1987. UMI 8809388.

Markard, A. Kurt Jooss and his work. *Ballet Review*, 1982, pp. 15–67.

—— & Markard, H. *Jooss: Dokumentation von Anna und Hermann Markard*. Koln: Ballett-Buhnen-Verlag, 1985.

Marriett, J. *Labanotation score of A Ball in Old Vienna*. Notated in 1976. New York: Dance Notation Bureau.

Martin, J. Art of Jooss. *The New York Times*, November 5, 1933.

Miesel, V. *Voices of German Expressionism*. Englewood Cliffs, New Jersey: Prentice-Hall, 1970.

Myers, B.S. *The German Expressionists: a generation in revolt*. New York: Praeger, 1956.

Odom, S.L. Wigman at Hellerau. *Ballet Review*, 1986, 14, 41–53.

Otte-Betz, I. The work of Rudolf von Laban. *Dance Observer*, December 1938, p. 147.

——. The work of Rudolf von Laban II. *Dance Observer*, January 1939, pp. 161–162.

——. The work of Rudolf von Laban III. *Dance Observer*, March 1939, pp. 189–190.

Preston-Dunlop, V. & S. Lauhausen (Eds.). *Schrifttanz a view of German Dance in the Weimar Republic*. London: Dance Books, 1990.

Prevost, N. Zurich, Dada and dance: formative ferment. *Dance Research Journal*, 1985, 17, 3–8.

Raabe, P. (Ed.). *The era of German Expressionism* (J.M. Ritchie, trans.). New York: The Overlook Press, 1974. (Originally published, 1965.)

Ritchie, J.M. *German Expressionist drama*. Boston: Twayne Publishers, 1976.

Samuel, R. & Thomas R.H. *Expressionism in German life, literature and the theatre*. Philadelphia: Albert Saifer, 1971.

Scheyer, E. The shapes of space: the art of Mary Wigman and Oskar Schlemmer. *Dance Perspectives 41*, 1970.

Schlemmer, T. (Ed.). *The letters and diaries of Oskar Schlemmer* (K. Winston, trans.). Middletown, Connecticut: Wesleyan University Press, 1972.

Schlicher, S. *TanzTheater Traditionen und Freiheiten Pina Bausch, Gerhard Bohner, Reinhild Hoffmann, Hans Kresni, Susanne Linke Rohwolt, Taschenbuch Verlag GmbH: Reinbek bei Hamburg, 1987.*

Schneede, U.M. *George Grosz: the artist in his society* (R. Kimber, trans.). New York: Barron's, 1985.

Schumacher, G. *Labanotation score of Pavane on the Death of an Infanta*. Notated in 1981. New York:

Dance Notation Bureau.

——. *Labanotation score of The Green Table*. Notated in 1980–1982. New York: Dance Notation Bureau.

Servos, N. Dance and Emancipation: the Wuppertal Dance Theater. *Ballet International*, January 1982, pp. 50–61.

Sorell, W. (Ed.). *Dance in its time*. Garden City: Doubleday, 1981.

——. *The dance has many faces* (2nd ed.). New York: Columbia University Press, 1966.

——. *The dancer's image: points and counterpoints*. New York: Columbia University Press, 1971.

——. (Ed. and trans.). *The Mary Wigman book*. Middletown, Connecticut: Wesleyan University Press, 1971.

——. Kurt Jooss on mime: the meaning of steps. *The Dancing Times*, July 1943, pp. 455–456.

Terry W. *Interview with Kurt Jooss*. Phonotape, 1967. Dance Collection of the New York Public Library at Lincoln Center.

——. The Jooss Ballet. *New York Herald Tribune*, September 28, 1941.

Thornton, S. *Laban's theory of movement, a new perspective*. Boston: Plays Inc., 1971.

Tobias, T. Bad dreams: Pina Bausch and her Tanztheater Wuppertal. *New York Magazine*, July 25, 1988, p. 54.

——. *Interview with Kurt Jooss*. Transcript of tape recording, September 26, 1976. Oral history project of the Dance Collection of The New York Public Library at Lincoln Center.

Tonnelat, E. Teutonic Mythology. In *New Larousse Encyclopedia of Mythology*. New York: Hamlyn, 1978.

Topaz, M. & Wile, C. *Labanotation score of The Green Table*. Notated in 1977. New York: Dance Noation Bureau.

Tucholsky, K. *What if? Satirical writings of Kurt Tucholsky* (H. Zohn & K.F. Ross, Eds. and trans.). New York: Funk and Wagnall, 1967.

——. Kurt Jooss on mime: the meaning of steps. *The Dancing Times*, July 1943, pp. 455–45.

Volkonsky, S.M. Ballets Jooss. *The Dancing Times*, April 1938, pp. 25–26.

Wigman, M. *The Language of dance* (W. Sorell, trans.). Middletown, Connecticut: Wesleyan University Press, 1966.

Willett, J. *Art and politics in the Weimar period: the new sobriety 1917–1933*. New York: Pantheon Books, 1978.

——. *Expressionism*. New York: McGraw-Hill, 1970.

——. *The Weimar years: a culture cut short*. New York: Abbeville Press, 1984.

Winerals, J. *Modern dance: The Jooss-Leeder method*. London: A.C. Black, 1958.

Wingler, H.M. *The Bauhaus* (W. Jabs & J. Stein, trans.). Cambridge: The MIT Press, 1984. (Originally published, 1962.)

Choreography and Dance
1993, Vol. 3, Part 2, pp. 25-43
Photocopying permitted by license only

The West German dance theatre
Paths from the twenties to the present

Suzanne Schlicher

"Much of what influences us, we come to know indirectly."

In the twentieth century the dance theatre of Kurt Jooss has been crucial to the renewed awareness of the shared traditions of dance and theatre. Jooss transformed Rudolf von Laban's analytical movement theories into a dance theatre that was effective and realistic, in marked contrast with the soloistic and expressionistic dance form of Mary Wigman. Jooss's renewal and expansion of content and movement language in the expressionistic dance of the 1920's gained importance from the reawakening of the West German dance theatre in the 1960's. The Folkwang Dance Department, founded in 1927 and led for decades by co-founder Kurt Jooss, has become since the 1960's the creative home for successive generations of young dancers and choreographers. Since 1945 the artistic development of dance in both Germanys has been marked by the conflict between the continuation of the modern Laban-Jooss tradition and a renewed classical ballet establishment.

KEY WORDS   Kurt Jooss, Rudolf von Laban, Jooss-Leeder, Folkwang, German dance, dance theatre, Tanztheater.

I. The tradition of autonomy

A constant aspect of European theatre in the twentieth century is a repeated widening and renewal of theatrical language, dramatic method and visual-spatial thinking. I would like to treat the development of the West German dance theatre in the same way, as a continual process of renewal and expansion, from Laban's theoretical and practical foundations, through Jooss's presentation of dance drama and his pedagogical work at the Folkwang School, to the appearance and international success of the Folkwang choreographers Pina Bausch, Reinhild Hoffmann and Susanne Linke.

The turn of the century set the stage for this century of continual change. It was a time of radical upheaval and awakening in every respect, politically, socially, and also artistically. In theatre and literature the names of Wsewolod E. Meyerhold, Antonin Artaud, Erwin Piscator and Bertolt Brecht, as well as the stage reforms initiated by Adolphe Appia and Edward Gordon Craig, mark the important stages. In dance the corresponding names include Emile Jaques Dalcroze and again Adolphe Appia with their collaborative work in the School for Rhythmic Gymnastics in Dresden-Hellerau, Rudolf von Laban and Kurt Jooss with their endeavours to create a dramatic dance theatre, and finally Oskar Schlemmer with his concept of man in space.

Loss of traditions after 1945.

I feel very homeless here in Germany. I miss the fact that there is no such thing as a tradition. I once thought that it would be an advantage not to have any fathers. But I have now realized that it is a great privation.[1]

Gerhard Bohner

The question of a tradition, of connecting lines leading from the start of the century down to us today, obviously raises the question of a so-called artistic heritage. In West German theatre and culture after 1945, many of the avant-garde tendencies and the emerging energies of the turn of the century were lost for a while. The aesthetics after 1945 worked contrary to those before 1933, rather than counting as their continuation—at least in the official State theatres and cultural enterprises. Only in the sixties and with a new "young" generation was there a turn back toward the developments of the twenties and a rediscovery of the critical theatre tradition. Documentary theatre and production theatre pointed the way in literature and on the stage. Meanwhile, a young generation of dancers and choreographers took a stand against the classical ballet establishment that had definitively prevailed on West German stages after the international successes of John Cranko and his Stuttgart company. New tendencies from the USA—pop culture, happenings, performance art, popular multimedia spectacles—confirmed such young choreographers as Hans Kresnik and Gerhard Bohner in their "anti-art" attitude. The choreographers Bausch, Hoffman and Linke, however, unlike their colleagues, began to draw their motivation from the productive climate of the tradition-rich Folkwang School, rather than from confrontation with an inflexible theatre establishment.

The West German dance theatre later rediscovered its tradition of modern dance, expressive dance and dance gymnastics, a tradition that had been lost and even deliberately pushed aside after 1945. Only in the seventies did the dance theories and writings of Laban and the dance theatre of Jooss come into focus once again as a German dance tradition—partly indeed because of the successes being won by the contemporary dance theatre descended from those two lines.

Forgetfulness and suppression of the modern German dance tradition also marked the ballet politics of East Germany after 1945. The exclusive orientation toward Soviet ballet aesthetics and pedagogy that was required, and also the doctrine of "socialist realism", fitted very poorly with the individualism, free improvisation and process-oriented work of the exponents of expressive dance. It is true that the Palucca School, rich in tradition, continued to operate in Dresden after 1945. Now that professional dance classes are no longer offered at the Lola Rogge School in Hamburg (formerly a Laban school), the Palucca School and the dance department of the Folkwang School in Essen are today the only German training academies for dance professionals that are rooted in German expressive dance. The training program in Dresden, however, was primarily geared toward a purely classical and academic dance career, far more so than has been the case at the Folkwang School for decades. Improvisation, the preferred instructional subject of Gret Palucca (a "persona non grata" in East Germany), was tolerated only as an auxiliary subject.

The tradition of autonomy

I studied in Essen with Kurt Jooss. What was exceptional about him was that he opened things up. Folkwang is not a school that teaches one specific technique. There were various techniques: classical, modern, European folk dance. Following my studies there I came to know other techniques and much else besides. But one is influenced not only by dance technique. Much of what influences us we come to know indirectly. What connects me with Jooss is human things, is his humanity.[2]

Pina Bausch

The work and influence of the choreographer Kurt Jooss are closely interwoven with the Folkwang School, the school that he co-founded in 1927 and whose history he helped to create as head of the Folkwang Dance Division for decades. Folkwang was unlike most of the private dance schools that were founded by independent modern dancers in the early years of the century, usually serving to finance the artistic work of the founder or his group as well as to provide instruction to amateurs. The Folkwang Dance Division was rather independent of the personal fate of its leader, since it was tied to a general school for art, theatre and music and operated under municipal administration.

These institutional provisions turned out to give the school a chance for survival in the era of fascism in Germany. While many modern schools were closed and their teachers forbidden to give lessons, in Essen the Dance Division was able to carry on as before, as a part of the Folkwang School, even after the emigration of Kurt Jooss in 1933. Leadership was provided by Albrecht Knust and Trude Pohl, students of Laban and Jooss. Thus Jooss was able once again to take up the work he had begun in the late 1920's upon his return to the school in 1949. This deliberate connection with the city administration became a far-sighted piece of good fortune for the preservation of the turn-of-the-century awakening and the modern dance of the Weimar Republic. The re-injection of their energies into the development of dance in Germany lead to the dance theatre of the seventies.

Theatrical dance versus free dance

Kurt Jooss, born in 1901, pupil of Rudolf von Laban, was active from the mid-twenties onward as a choreographer, artistic director, ballet master and teacher. His works that remain most successful to the present day: *The Green Table* and *Big City*, date from the year 1932, while *Pavane on the Death of an Infanta*, also still performed today, was created three years earlier. Jooss established himself at a time when the great revolutionary surges of modern expressionistic theatre and dance had already been displaced or even superseded by such tendencies as the New Objectivity and the New Search for Form. The young choreographer was thus able to give new precision to the overly effusive ideas of the turn of the century, and to make them more concrete for the sake of practical employment in theatre and dance. To this end he also brought together the energies of the dance gymnastics and body culture movements of the twenties and thirties, and the aesthetic innovations of theatre, film, and expressionistic cinema. He was the one artist who could integrate the various media and avant-garde tendencies of his time. His dance drama *The Green Table* makes exemplary use of the novel stage lighting effects of the modern theatre and the dramatic principles of film production. Scenic montage and the collage principle were tried out in the new dance theatre; simultaneity of scenic action on the stage was realized by adapting cinematic methods and panoramic stage lighting.

In excluding the solo dance and the movement choir, Jooss's concern was to revive theatrical dance as a respected and autonomous theatre art, the equal in value and acceptance of any other. With his dance dramas, a new form of action ballet, he established the dramatic expressive power of modern dance as a language for setting forth contemporary commitments and thematic statements. Turning aside from the emotional astonishment, individualized movement experience and cosmic worldviews that had been the urgent creative concerns of solo dance and movement choirs, Jooss's dance theatre undertook the mediation of and confrontation with social reality and actuality.

The artistic position of Jooss turned out to be even more important for the development of German dance in the postwar decades because of the fact that Rudolf von Laban, unlike Jooss, did not return to Germany from his exile in England. The active and direct transmission of the Laban tradition to the theatrical dance of West Germany occurred almost exclusively through the person and work of his student Kurt Jooss.

The basis of Jooss's dance theatre in Laban's concept of dance

Laban gave us a great gift: an understanding of every kind of movement and a broad view of the entire movement complex. We were youngsters at the time, hungry for experience and movement. Classical dancing had little to offer us then, because we rightly felt that it was too one-sided. Laban came at precisely the right moment with his movement analysis. He opened our eyes and loosened our limbs; he opened up a complete artistic domain for us to work in.[3]

Kurt Jooss

Jooss met Laban in 1920 when he was still a drama student. He was immediately fascinated by Laban as a person and by his chosen field, the modern dance. As a young and committed student of Laban, he followed him in 1921 from Stuttgart to Mannheim, where he came in contact with the theatrical establishment. Laban was working there as ballet master and choreographer for the municipal theatre. He undertook the experiment of combining his own small company with the established classical corps de ballet, in a mutually fructifying dance ensemble—an attempt that was admittedly not very successful. In Mannheim, Jooss took the stage as a young soloist in several works by Laban, and he came to know both the possibilities and the artistic hindrances and prejudices of the theatrical enterprise.

The third place where they worked together was Hamburg, where Jooss was a member of the *Tanzbühne Laban*. Laban, in addition to his voluminous activity as a choreographer, formed his first "lay movement choirs" there, opening up for his pupils and dancers new fields of activity and experience. During his time in Hamburg, Jooss, as a teacher and a movement regisseur, became very familiar with Laban's movement teaching and got to know both sides of Laban's creativity: monumental movement choirs and lay dance on the one hand, more subtle chamber dance creations under Laban's direction on the other. In addition, together with his colleague Sigurd Leeder, Jooss developed his own artistic ideas and methods. The two of them worked out a tour program, "Two Male Dancers," and broadened their dance language by also studying classical dance in Vienna, Paris and elsewhere.

In 1924 Jooss's appointment as 'movement regisseur' and as director of a dance company of his own at the Münster theatre set Jooss on his final path towards independence and in the direction of professional theatre work.

I needed independence for my further development, so with great regret I left the Tanzbühne Laban. At about the same time, the Tanzbühne Laban had to disband due to financial misfortunes on a Yugoslavian tour. I was able to collect some of the former members of my Neue Tanzbühne in Münster. From there, in three years we made a name for ourselves in Germany....[4]

Kurt Jooss

Nonetheless, the source of the theatrical work of Jooss remained the movement theory of Rudolf von Laban. From his new positions, first in Münster and then from 1927 on at the Folkwang School in Essen, Jooss followed closely the further development of Laban's writings on movement and his continuing exploration of the expressive qualities and spatial connections in dance, as formulated in the two new subjects of *Eukinetics* and *Choreutics*.

[In] the whole period from 1927 on,... we developed what was then called *Eukinetics*. Sigurd [Leeder] and I had been to Bad Mergentheim. That is where [Rudolf von] Laban had a summer course, the same year.... Sigurd and I—oh, now it becomes very dramatic—started notation, now coming and beginning. We had worked on notation the whole of the summer. Then, in August, we went with our results to Mergentheim.... when we arrived there, we found that they had just devised a kind of *Eukinetics* system—a system of, well, *how* to move.... I was tremendously impressed by this; I made it my special subject. And when we opened the Folkwang School in Essen that autumn, Sigurd did the *Choreutic* side of it and I the *Eukinetic*.... From then on, I was possessed by the idea of *Eukinetics* and the working of it. I worked it out for years with the students, learning more and more about it.... This developed and its peak, I think, was *The Green Table*. It is really the showpiece of *Eukinetics*]and also of *Choreutics*.[5]

Kurt Jooss

Laban and Jooss came together again in England. Laban had followed his former pupil into exile in 1936 in a roundabout way, after his schools were closed thoughout Germany when he fell out of favor with the new regime. Laban found a new home for his creativity in the Jooss-Leeder School of Dance at Dartington Hall, which became the base for his many-sided artistic, scientific and pedagogical activity for the next two decades in England.

The new dance theatre

The goal is always dance theatre, dance theatre understood as a form and technique of dramatic choreography with regard to its libretto, the music, and especially its performers. It means the further development in school and studio of new dance techniques toward impersonal objective methods of dramatic dance, and the gradual inclusion of traditional classical dance into the new discipline.[6]

Kurt Jooss

Laban based his concept of a new dance theatre on the possibilities and the experiences of stage reform and aesthetic innovation that arose in theatre, film and art at the beginning of the century. In *The World of the Dancer*, published in 1920, he had already formulated a set of concrete foundations for the dance theatre that remain valid to this day: the dancer, as a creative personality and an individual performer; the body, with its power of expression, its capacity for experience, and its multifaceted repertoire for movement as the autonomous bearer of meaning; movement, as three dimensional experience in space, that is as the principle of three dimensionality in space itself and in the performer contained within space; simplicity, in props and in costumes, and in the expressive power of empty space; finally, the audience, as an open, onlooking, associate participant in the performance, whose sense of movement must still be trained for the sake of "an experiment in seeing images and watching movement."

These requirements for aesthetic innovation in the dance were most consistently worked out in Kurt Jooss's choreography. In hindsight it is very much to Jooss's credit that he found it possible, in accepting the Laban inheritance, to separate Laban as theatre practicioner and movement researcher from Laban as mystical guru and world-redeeming philosopher. Laban's vocabulary of "festive culture", "mass soul", "sensing the world in dance", and "the healthy Nation", or even such nationalistic catch phrases as "German dance art" (a phrase also used by Mary Wigman), cannot be found in Jooss's work and thought. Laban's dream of collective cult festivals, his idealizations of communal feeling and rhythmic education, as well as the "back to nature" theme generally cultivated in expressive dance, were all set aside by Jooss with his decisive attachment to the stage and his alertness to the time he lived in and to contemporary art. His interests did not lie in large creations of mass edification or choral movement, but in "the directing, in the finest detail, of an ensemble of soloists, preferably no more than twenty persons."[7]

"Art wants and must have works"

Although their ways had parted, Laban and Jooss agreed in their estimation of the future and the necessity for modern dance. In public discussion they showed themselves to be fellow combatants on behalf of the art of theatrical dance and dramatic dance theatre. Frequently, for example at the second German Dance Congress in Essen, 1928, they took this stand in open contradiction to Mary Wigman, perhaps Laban's most prominent pupil, who consistently and vehemently defended free dance.

Laban knew very well, as did Jooss, the dangers of excessive subjectivism and total lack of form in soloistic expressive dance, and also the artistic limitations of his mass spectacles.

The 'phenomenon' of the dancer who dances himself, even when surrounded by a group, is fundamentally inartistic.... Art wants and must have works. Only the work in its completed, formally closed-up totality can speak to the general public and thus be in accord with the meaning of art.[8]

Rudolf von Laban

Both Laban and Jooss saw the inclusion of modern dance as a stage art within the state-supported theatrical institutions as a matter of survival, notwithstanding the artistic and structural compromises it entailed. As advocates of "objectivised artistic forms" (Laban) and a "creative" compromise between free personal expression and formal ties" (Jooss), they stood up for the new dance theatre:

The new dance theatre now has the task of finding all the possibilities of dance expression and of welding them together again into a synthesis. Whether this synthesis be called dance tragedy, dance comedy, or movement symphony, what is essential and valuable about it lies in the similarity with a musical or dramatic form, but above all in this characterictic of an objectivised artistic form: to be a work of art.[9]

Here Rudolf von Laban is sketching (in 1927, the year that the Folkwang School was founded) almost the exact path and goal that Jooss pursued consistently, in his work at the Folkwang School in the thirties, with the Folkwang Dance Theatre Studio founded there in 1928, and with his later private company, the Ballets Jooss.

II. Laban's movement analysis and Jooss's language of dance

In my opinion, the basic contribution that Leeder and Jooss made toward systematisation consists in the fact that they, following Laban, undertook a far-reaching and summarizing analysis of the basic factors of body movement. Their analysis of the biomechanical, dynamic, spatial and temporal aspects showed those factors to be closely connected and to work together, permanently and inseparably, with motivation, the psychic aspect.[10]

Patricio Bunster

Laban objectified the connection between internal experience and external expression, whereas expressive dance placed it in the center of the creative process. For Laban, expression and impression are equally authoritative configuring factors, "two distinct spatio-rhythmic conditions of the ego." He therefore treated the interdependent conditions of mental and physical stress as a reciprocal relationship between different tensions of form, or of the body.

The symbol contains within itself the power to excite, tension. It has the power to release excitement because of the sensory impression made by its form. The dancer has transferred a 'power of speech' from his gesture into a linear structure, by making that structure similar to the tensions that are active in his gesture. In this same way, objects whose contours or tension-forms are seen as similar to certain human gestures (be they gestures of conception, of feeling, or of the body) are seen as symbols of the excitement that lives within those gestures.[11]

Rudolf von Laban

Moreover, Laban also uncovered the entire sphere of movement as interaction, encompassing also the associated perceptive and receptive processes. Thus he provided a physiological and psychological basis for dance as an acceptable language of the theatre: communicative, calculable, and therefore goal-directed. This is exactly what we find realized on stage in Jooss's dance theatre.

In his Choreutics and Eukinetics Rudolf von Laban created the basis for an analysis of movement that embraces (in extensions not yet foreseeable) the classical in the same way as the newly created movement material. The underlying research into human movement with

Figure 1   Laban and Jooss 1938/39 in Dartington Hall (Jooss Archive).

regard to space and rhythm has brought to light a lawfulness that creates, with the force of natural simplicity, an unmistakeable criterion for the value or lack of value of a given movement in a given inner connection.[12]

Kurt Jooss

Jooss derived dramatic substance and the power to make statements from Laban's theoretical considerations. By giving his representative content the concreteness of body language, he fought against the prejudice of his time that dance should be exclusively an expression of feeling. Until then, the fascination of modern dance had mainly derived from the expressivity of body language. This was true also of many colleagues working in film and the spoken theatre. In contrast with this, Jooss's stylized language of gesture is characterized by a clear consciousness of the reciprocal dependence between the dramatic statement and the language of form and movement.

The idea of dance drama

The medium of the dance is the living human body with the power to convey ideas inherent in its movements.... In the dramatic dance ... these pure imaginings of movement are fused with the dramatic idea, and the fusion of the two elements creates a new entity, the dance drama, whose subject-matter is the thought of the creator crystallized into active and suffering human characters.[13]

Kurt Jooss

However clearly Jooss may have oriented himself by Laban's work, his dance-drama creations still show just as forcefully an independent attitude and include important new aspects. His dance theatre was a proving ground for content that was unfamiliar to the dance world of his day, and for new theatrical methods such as the drama of expressionistic stations or stages, and the principle of scenic montage. At the same time it oriented itself toward the aesthetic innovations and new staging possibilities of film-making and the expressionistic cinema.

Jooss's themes, such as his pacifism and his plea for a more humane world, also permeated the progressive art trends of his time, from literary expressionism to the films of Charlie Chaplin. Thanks to his artistic farsightedness and his overall openness and involvement, these themes were able to receive a direct dramatic translation into the medium of dance. One finds, in his dance dramas, figures typical of those in the art works of Otto Dix and George Grosz, and one senses a political awareness of the circumstances of the day that echoes the warnings of a Kurt Tucholsky. These themes—war, post-war trauma, metropolis, loneliness, the anguish of the outsiders, dictatorship and despotism—confirm his social involvement, an involvement as artist and as human being that brought him immediately into conflict with the regime of 1933 and drove him into exile.

Developing dance as language

Jooss himself left no teaching manual and expressed himself sparingly on his realistic dance language. But again and again one finds Jooss referring to Laban, pointing to the latter's deep-probing research interests and to the reciprocal dependence between "dance forms and behavior in general, especially the working habits of a given time."

This new 'language' of dancing which you use in your ballets is, if I may say so, our common work. And here I have to thank you for the lively flexibility with which you use the innumerable forms of movement which in a life-long work I have endeavoured to liberate from the influence of an empty tradition. I had always a notion that some day it would be possible to achieve that without dogmatic narrow-mindedness. You are striving in your new works towards a further development and deepening of dance expression, without making concessions either to the conventional pantomime or to excessive sentimentality.[14]

Rudolf von Laban, writing to Kurt Jooss

Laban had already emphasized that dance, as expressive gesture, should not be thought of as autonomous but as "remembered gesture"; it connects with the quite personal experiential background of the spectator, but also bears and reflects within its context a social meaning.

Yet the whole inheritance of the art of movement throughout history is so meager that it has hardly occurred to the great public that there is a connection between the changes of social life and dance.... A second outstanding characteristic of the contemporary art of movement is the congruity of the new forms of dance expression with the movement habits of modern man.[15]

Rudolf von Laban

In fact, Jooss made considerable use of typical and characteristic movement possibilities to be found in movement of the work place, from the social dancing of his time and also from historic dances with their specific body images. Like the later dance theatre choreographers of the seventies and eighties, Jooss "quoted" known and conventional movement material in order to make use of the social connotations and the meaning-associations connected with them. In *Pavane on the*

Death of an Infanta (1929), Jooss invoked the court pavane as a movement picture of the world of the Spanish court, smothered under rules and conventions. The mechanical sharpness and inviolability with which each step was precisely articulated with every gesture and head movement placed, allowed Jooss to characterize the severity and accuracy of the court ceremonial, which he contrasted with the freely composed, softly flowing step sequence that depicted the childish Infanta. In *Big City* (1932) Jooss made use of the disparate social meanings of the Charleston and the Valse Musette to characterize the gulf between the social strata represented in the two dance halls.

"The familiar shall become the known"

Jooss achieved a directness and simplicity in the language of movement and the method of dance theatre that fairly represents the material without cozying up to it or being a merely naturalistic milieu study. His central humanistic gaze was focussed on the gestures and movement habits of his characters. He bared the central derivation of the movements and depicted the social surroundings of his characters by using a movement system derived from their everyday life and milieu. The everyday movements used by Jooss in his dance dramas never reduce to movement in isolation; as presented on stage, their linkage with the social context has always been clear or apparent. This linkage was always the source for his methods of expression in dance theatre; it also forms a significant connection with the dance theatre of the seventies and eighties. Like Jooss, these recent choreographers attain concreteness or contemporaneity and realism by presenting the social character of people's public and private behavior. Their dance pieces have, as central themes, social role-images, norms of conduct, and body language communication signals. Brecht's motto—"The familiar shall become the known"—is now being realized primarily in the sphere of body language communication. Bodily stances and bodily conduct have social relevance and make statements on the underlying issues. The dance theatre of Pina Bausch became a model for using the social relevance of bodily stances and bodily conduct on stage.

"Everything is routine...."

Why do we dance at all. It is quite dangerous how far this has developed at present or in recent years. Everything is routine and nobody knows any more why people move.[16]

Pina Bausch

Jooss's insistence that "Every movement shall have a meaning" still contains a belief in the formative power of a purely dance-like method or expression. The contemporary dance theatre is committed to a search for the WHY, for honesty in body language expression. This led to a recognition that a language of exclusively dance-like forms may involve a loss of meaning and empty symbolism. It also led to a repudiation of any kind of closure or claimed aesthetic harmony for a work of art. The traditional belief of Laban and Jooss in simplicity, in reduction, in movement as the chief means of making a statement, is often reformulated in the dance theatre of today as questions, doubts, and even distrust of enthusiasms with technique and body or movement cults, both in daily life and on the stage.

This conflict provokes a radicalism in the work of art, in the performance and in the performers themselves. In their endless repetitions of a segmented movement language, choreographers and works from the contemporary dance theatre are questioning how physical effort and psychic striving can be brought together at all in dance today. On the far side of a frightening virtuosity of productive capacity that is seen today on the stage as well as in reality, choreographers such as Pina Bausch, Susanne Linke and Gerhard Bohner are searching for another kind of truth and beauty in dance, one hidden behind objects and bodies. Their works can be read as a continuing effort toward the honesty of a language of form and movement that will never again compromise its starkly presented excerpts of reality by imposing a new harmony upon them.

Jooss's contribution to renewing and expanding the references to content in the expressive dance of the twenties lies in his critical reflective analysis of his time and its underlying conditions. His vision was critical, like that of the theatre and cinema of the day. In the twenties, the Austro-Hungarian author Ödön von Horváth called himself "the true chronicler of his time." This self-definition can also be applied to the authors of dance theatre, from Jooss to the present. Like Horváth, the choreographers of the contemporary dance theatre see a direct expression of the broken emotional world that their stage characters inhabit in the banality and triviality of everyday life, of everyday gestures and postures. Whether we take Chaplin's slapstick films, Horváth's folk legends, Jooss's dance dramas or the pictorial worlds of a Pina Bausch, we find that the realism of their epic theatre and their technique of representation exhausts itself neither in movement language nor in content simply reproduced. Their realistic-humanistic analysis takes the hidden statements of both the linguistic and the body language domains to be the most revealing expression of inner truth.

"We have a duty at the theatre: human problems, authority, power—to show all of that.... The best example is *The Green Table* by Kurt Jooss"[17] (Hans Kresnik). To develop dance as a language was the lifelong credo of Kurt Jooss. This attitude may define the intersection of three historic efforts: Laban's movement analysis, grounded in the observation of everyday and work place movements; the Jooss dance theatre with its realistic, communicative language of dance; and the contemporary dance theatre (not limited to the Folkwang choreographers) with its attempt to connect once again with the critical-humanistic tradition of the Weimar theatre.

III. Master classes in dance

The Folkwang School is a good training ground; we had time, and we could take time. The first choreography that was done there grew quite slowly, and that is good too, because then the success is also steady and long. The Folkwang Dance Studio is very good that way: one can really try things out, and many people have done so there.[18]

Susanne Linke

For three decades the Folkwang School and its associated choreographic studio have been a breeding ground for the rising generation of choreographers and performers. Unlike the Ballet Studio (later, the Dance Forum) of Cologne, that city's home for new generation choreographers, where Hans Kresnik and

Figure 2   *Schritte verfolgen*—Susanne Linke (Photo: Gert Weigelt).

Gerhard Bohner presented their first works in the 1960's, the Folkwang School and Studio are distinguished by the continuity of their attention to the rising generation of choreographers. Pina Bausch, Reinhild Hoffmann and Susanne Linke all did their training in dance and choreography there, and succeeded one another in directing the Studio: Bausch from 1969 to 1973, Reinhild from 1975 to 1978, and Linke from 1975 to 1985.

The groundwork for the successful nurture of new talent at Folkwang was laid by Kurt Jooss. Reappointed as Director of the Dance Division upon his return to West Germany in 1949, he introduced the so-called "Master Classes in Dance".

Hidden behind this title was a small dance ensemble of eight to ten members, some of them recent graduates and others already experienced dancers. Among those whom Jooss was able to attract for this Folkwang Ballet, as the ensemble called itself on tours, was Pina Bausch, one of his most talented students, who returned to Germany after having spent several years in the United States.

The project of master classes for dance was a complete novelty in German dance history. Jooss's concept was to let young dancers mature through productive ensemble work with an internationally oriented modern repertory, and to stimulate their choreographic creativity in cooperative undertakings with renowned teachers and choreographers working in diverse styles. The intention in offering this one or two year program of advanced study was to make it easier for dancers to make the leap to a larger state theatre or to a career as a soloist. Work was carried on in professional conditions comparable to those of the performing theatre, but free of the fixed schedule of premieres and openings. During the 1962–63 season, Antony Tudor rehearsed the company in *Jardin aux Lilas* and *Little Improvisations*, Lucas Hoving of the José Limón Company also brought his choreographic works to Essen, most notably *Songs of Encounter* (1962). Jooss worked on several new pieces and rehearsed the young company in revivals of *The Green Table* and *Pavane on the Death of an Infanta*. The Folkwang Ballet went on several national and international tours, and in 1964 became the first dance company from West Germany to give a guest performance in East Germany.

Re-establishment of modern dance and dance theatre

Even before the founding of the Folkwang Studio, Jooss had practiced an uncommon openness toward the international developments in modern dance. Already in 1956 the Folkwang School gave a series of events entitled "Dance and Ballet in America". In 1959 the first European-American summer course in contemporary dance took place at the Folkwang School, with Pearl Lang, Alfredo Corvino and others as lecturers. In 1960 Yuriko Kikuchi followed, and Jooss and Tudor gave a joint seminar in choreographic composition. All of these events gave important opportunities to the young choreographers and dancers of the Folkwang School. Both Hans Kresnik and Gerhard Bohner, dance theatre choreographers initially located in Cologne and Berlin, developed their dance theatre methods in reaction against the classical dance aesthetics whose vocabulary and repertoire they knew well, as soloists of great ballet companies. The Folkwang choreographers, on the other hand, based their formative explorations on European and American modern dance.

In that decade the Folkwang Ballet was the only active professional modern dance company in West Germany, and one of the very few that existed in all of Europe. In a German dance landscape that was otherwise classically dominated, it offered working possibilities and an opportunity for growth to qualified modern dancers from within the country and from abroad.

Jean Cébron, a student of Sigurd Leeder who is today Professor of Modern Dance at the Folkwang School, also worked as a dancer and choreographer at the Folkwang Dance Studio in the 1960's. His unconventional abstract-modern choreography was too unusual to be performed in the city-sponsored theatres of the day, but intensive collaboration with Cébron was an important influence on the young dancer Pina Bausch. In 1967 she presented *Fragment*, her first

Figure 3   Rehearsal for *Lilac Garden* (Photo: Michael Diekamp).

choreography; just two years later her second piece, *In the Winds of Time*, performed by the Folkwang company, won the first prize at the Choreographic Competition in Cologne.

Only at the end of the 1960's, with the establishment of the contemporary dance theatre, did the one track nature of the German dance landscape open up. The first dance theatre company was formed in 1968, when Hans Kresnik was engaged by the Bremen Theatre. This was followed by the Tanz-Forum Cologne (1971), the Dance Theatre of Darmstadt under the direction of Gerhard Bohner (1972), and the Wuppertal Dance Theatre under the direction of Pina Bausch (1973).

The Folkwang Dance Studio in its third decade

It is not just the Folkwang School and Jooss's work there that can be described retrospectively as the cradle of the German dance theatre; above all it is the time itself of the Folkwang Ballet in the 1960's under the direction of Jooss. The departure of Jooss from the School in 1968, and the acceptance by Pina Bausch of the direction of the Studio in the following year, mark the beginnings of a new stage in the history of the Folkwang Dance Studio. It became an increasingly essential forum and testing ground for young choreographers in Germany and from abroad, and has remained so to the present day. In the 1980's a second and third generation of young choreographers drew attention to themselves, including Marileen Breuker (now working in France), Christine Brunel (a freelance choreographer in Essen today), Mitsuro Sasaki and Urs Dietrich, choreographer and dance partner of Susanne Linke.

In Germany today, apart from the Folkwang School and its Dance Studio, only the Noverre Company of Stuttgart still fosters new talent in choreography consistently and successfully. Such people as Jirí Kylián, William Forsythe and John Neumeier have had their first works performed there. The only formal course of study in choreography is located at the Leipzig Academy, and so far it has primarily trained choreographers in the lay dance methods that were greatly favored in the former East Germany.

In addition to supplying constant new discoveries in choreography, the Folkwang Dance Studio has also trained many of the dancers in the dance theatre companies of Pina Bausch and Reinhild Hoffmann. Today, owing to the enormous international success of the German dance theatre, the Folkwang School as well as the Folkwang Dance Studio are a great attraction for dancers from the whole world, especially from Spain, Italy and South America.

Pina Bausch has been the director for several years. Alongside Jean Cébron there is also Lutz Forster, who holds a professorship in modern dance. He is a member of the Wuppertal Dance Theatre, and was for several years a co-director of the José Limón Company. Dancers from the Bausch Company also teach at the school.

The open and artistically helpful climate at the Folkwang School, with its close community of the various trainir; departments and arts under one roof—dance, drama, music, opera, photograp.y, graphic design—is always praised by Folkwang choreographers and teachers as extremely helpful and stimulating for creative work. Interdisciplinary training for performing artists may be a matter of course in the United States. For Germany however, where academies for music, theatre and dance were set up after the second World War in complete isolation from one another spatially, organizationally and in subject matter, the Folkwang School is an exception.

Elbowroom for finding one's own way

"Jooss and Graham don't go together," declares Hans Züllig, who had danced for many years with the Ballets Jooss and who followed Jooss as Director of the Folkwang Dance Division. This difference is also stressed by Jean Cébron, Professor of Modern Dance at the Folkwang School and training director of the dance theatre companies of Pina Bausch and Reinhild Hoffmann. Cébron, following Jooss and Züllig, is the current generation's embodiment of the Folkwang teaching tradition. He builds mainly on the instructional combinations of Jooss and Leeder in shaping the spatial and dynamic thinking of his students. Another influence conveyed through the teaching of Cébron flows from his particular knowledge of the classical Cecchetti technique. Cébron's work thus keeps alive the great Folkwang tradition of maintaining stylistic independence while at the same time absorbing new elements.

Without Mary Wigman I would not be what I am today. But without the Folkwang Dance School I would not be that either. The Folkwang School gave me bread, gave me reason and reality. Mary Wigman gave me everything else; she gave me life.[19]

Susanne Linke

Even though Jooss failed to realize his goal of codifying a reliable modern dance technique based on a synthesis of classical academic dance with Laban's spatial doctrines of movement and choreography, the methodical attempts at movement creation by Laban, Jooss and Leeder with their continuation in Cébron's work allow us to recognize a kind of systematization that could not be achieved in the case of other teaching traditions, e.g. Wigman's. The so-called "Wigman technique," mainly talked about abroad, is usually disputed and criticized by her students in Germany because of its emphasis on what is individual, merely

Figure 4 *Poème dansé*—Cebron and Bausch (Photo: Michael Diekamp).

personal. In the Jooss-Leeder tradition the instructional combinations are always understood to be small choreographies that provide training in compositional thinking. Jooss wanted to make his students keenly aware of the breadth of variation and the many possibilities of articulation of a movement. In the instruction given by Mary Wigman, as her students continue to stress, the HOW was more important and influential than the WHAT, and the uniqueness of dance was in the forefront. Jooss's inquiry into the psychological content of movement with regard to space, dynamics and rhythm pointed to the idea that expression in human movement was analyzable, an idea which Wigman, that great champion of free dance (though she too was a Laban student), took to be suspect or at least not yet practicable in her art and her teaching.

Apart from questions of style and technique, the search for truth in expression and radical self-examination indicates an intersection of the tradition with the choreographic work in dance theatre today. The self-reliance of the Folkwang tradition gave to the Jooss students Bausch, Hoffmann and Linke, and to the generation of Folkwang choreographers who followed them, a certain independence and self-assurance in dealing with the various influences they encountered, from the American modern dance of Graham, through Cunningham, to the latest developments and fashions of post modernism and the New Dance. It saved them from any unilateral adopting of American dance techniques, and guaranteed them aesthetic freedom and stylistic independence.

IV. "When does one call it Dance?"

It is simply the question of where it starts to be dance, where not. Where is the beginning? When does one call it dance? No doubt it has something to do with consciousness, with body consciousness and how one shapes something. But it does not need to have this kind of aesthetic form; it can be something quite different and still be dance.[20]

Pina Bausch

The Polish theatre critic Andrzej Wirth speaks of looking at things "on the formal plane" when dealing with the enormous impact of Bertolt Brecht on the theatre of today. In a similar way, one can speak of the impact of the Jooss dance theatre as being on an essentially formal plane. Above all, Pina Bausch transfers the structural principles of Jooss's choreography into the scenic sequence of her images. Laws of spatial and dynamic composition, elsewhere used mainly to determine the flow of steps and the sequences of movement and motive, come to define the total dynamics of form and content. The steps and scenic elements of the piece behave like individual movements or movement elements in a polyphonic choreography: each little mosaic stone is retained, remembered, reflected by the next. This method of choreographic composition leads in the end to a structured formal totality for the piece. Thus in a work of dance theatre by a Bausch, Hoffmann or Linke it makes no difference whether these mosaic stones are single movements or step sequences, a scenic action or a complex theatrical scene—taken even further: a musical element, a prop, a fragment of speech. . . . The only decisive thing is the structural pertinence of the material, its meaning associations within the choreography.

Scenic collage and polyphonic composition

Jooss's choreographic phrasing of movements, Laban's image of the counterplay of lability and stability, also his principle of dynamic tension contrasts, are reshaped in the dance theatre of a Reinhild Hoffman. They become a theatre of movement in which time, space and dynamics are used as dramaturgical patterns in the composition, scene sequences and rhythms of the work. Each piece constructs its own rhythm. This also applies to Pina Bausch's works, which mirror the principles of Laban and Jooss most clearly in their scenic collage thinking and polyphonic composition:

> She has a wonderful mastery of polyphonics. The way she fills a stage, then empties it—I think that the usual audience doesn't even perceive it, but it is amazing how fluid it is: first one dancer enters, then at the proper instant the next.
> Pina Bausch has something that many others do not have. Despite collage, despite its almost spotty quality, her work always has a musical line.... With many others this ends in confusion, because someone enters in the wrong place or at the wrong time. It's like an abstract painter who paints only one spot. It comes down to this: one painter places it in such a way that a tension springs up; another places it where it just remains a silly spot.[21]

Hans Züllig

The scenic autonomy in which various individual actions take place at the same time, and also the autonomy of the various theatrical means such as music, stage space, scenery and choreography, has one of its starting-points in Jooss's polyphonic method of composition, in his structural exploitation of the multi-rhythmic possibilities of the body and the free association and dissociation of the rhythms of body, composition and music. Brecht's separation of elements and Jooss's method of free composition are combined in the contemporary dance theatre, especially in the main structural principle of montage, with its requirement that a stringent formal structure should maintain the dramatic narrative or the psychological action in the absence of all linear logic. That "action should be valued as tension," that the idea of dance theatre should be understood not as a "raw happening" but rather as a coexistence of tensions, opposed tensions, expectations and resolutions, was already posited by Laban in 1920. The dramaturgy of montage gives the dance theatre of today its characteristic freedom of dissonances and a multifarious fragility in performance.

"... in the language of an entirely new art"

Apart from its concrete influences within dance, the Jooss legacy has an important integrative aspect for the choreographers of dance theatre, regardless of their training or background: openness toward related art forms, in particular the crossing of all frontiers that divide the theatrical arts from one another. In the twentieth century the Jooss dance theatre marked a decisive stage in the renewed awareness of the common lines of tradition in dance history and in theatre history. Both the Jooss dance theatre and the dance theatre of the present should be viewed as standing in a close reciprocal relationship with the aesthetic innovations then and now in the kindred disciplines, especially the spoken theatre, film, and experimental stage design. And always there is the return to the deepest sources of originality in man, as Rudolf von Laban emphasized:

My dear Jooss,

It gave me great pleasure before my departure from Dartington to watch some of the rehearsals of your two new ballets. I found confirmed what we have both known for a long time: namely, that although your work has developed in an individual and original manner, its source is as clear and its enthusiasm as genuine as it was when I had the privilege to introduce you to the Noble Art of Dancing.

And that means much, not only of personal satisfaction to myself, but to the dance in general. I see how through your work, more than through the work of any of my other disciples and collaborators, a great hope nears fulfillment: that the language of movement might become apt to express in an easily understandable form those deep and essential things which can only be stated by dance....

I am well aware that you would resent being called the apostle of some new School of Thought; but you have to admit, since you have proved it again with your latest works, that you are a poet who can give utterance to the eternal ideas of humanity as well as to the problems of our own day in the language of an entirely new art.[22]

Rudolf von Laban, writing to Kurt Jooss

Notes

1. Gerhard Bohner, quoted by Hartmut Regitz, "Ein choreographischer Einzelgaenger. Das aktuelle Portrait: Gerhard Bohner", *Ballett Journal/Das Tanzarchiv*, June 1985, p. 73.
2. Pina Bausch, "Der Tanz muss etwas ganz Erwachsenes werden," conversation with Helmut Scheier, *Jahrbuch Ballett 1986—Tanz-theater*, p. 26.
3. Kurt Jooss, quoted in *Die Welt*, January 24 1977.
4. Kurt Jooss, "Autobiographical Note," in Anna Markard, "Kurt Jooss and His Work", *Ballet Review*, Spring 1982, p. 18.
5. Kurt Jooss, "The Green Table—A Dance of Death" interview with Michael Huxley, *Ballett International*, Cologne, August–September 1982, pp. 8–9.
6. Kurt Jooss, "Development of my Work in Outline," 1955. Manuscript in the Jooss Archives, Wiesbaden.
7. Kurt Jooss to Niedecken-Gebhard, April 2 1935, in the Niedecken-Gebhard nachlass collection, Theatre Museum of the University of Cologne-zu-Wahn.
8. Rudolf von Laban, "Tanztheater und Bewegungschor," in *Laban*, Die Tanzarchiv-Reihe volume 19/20. Cologne: Verlag Das Tanzarchiv, 1979, p. 3.
9. Ibid., p. 2.
10. Patricio Bunster, "... so interessant wie das Leben," *Theater der Zeit* (Berlin), October 1984, p. 30.
11. Rudolf von Laban, *Die Welt des Tänzers*. Stuttgart: Walter Seifert Verlag, 1920, p. 40.
12. Kurt Jooss, "Tanz in der Mitte des Jahrhunderts," *Musik der Zeit: Ballettheft* (Bonn and London), 1952, p. 10.
13. Kurt Jooss, quoted in A.V. Coton, *The New Ballet, Kurt Jooss and his Work*. London: Dennis Dobson, 1946, p. 29.
14. Rudolf von Laban to Kurt Jooss: in program notes dated Christmas 1938, Jooss Archives, Wiesbaden.
15. Rudolf von Laban, *Modern Educational Dance*. London: Macdonald & Evans Ltd., 1975, pp. 2–3.
16. Pina Bausch, "Ein Interview," conversation with Jochen Schmidt, in Hedwig Muller/ Norbert Servos, *Pina Bausch—Wuppertaler Tanz-theater* (Cologne: Ballett-Buhnen-Verlag, 1979), unpaginated.
17. Johann Kresnik, "Wir müssen nachdenklich machen," *Jahrbuch Ballett 1986—Tanztheater*, p. 37.
18. Susanne Linke, conversation with the author, June 29 1986.
19. Susanne Linke, conversation with the author, June 29 1986.
20. Pina Bausch, "Ein Interview," cited in Note 16.
21. Hans Züllig, conversation with the author, July 14 1986.
22. Rudolf von Laban to Kurt Jooss, cited in Note 14.

Choreography and Dance
1993, Vol 3, Part 2, pp. 45-51
Photocopying permitted by license only

Jooss the teacher

His pedagogical aims and the development of the choreographic principles of harmony

Anna Markard

The break away from tradition produced a new dance in Europe based on natural movement and free rhythm. Rudolf von Laban was a great stimulating force and his findings of "the principles of movement" and the "laws of space" were developed by some of his disciples in individual ways. Kurt Jooss became instrumental in developing and applying these discoveries for the professional theater. In 1927 Jooss established the Folkwangschule in Essen and introduced a curriculum based on Laban's Choreographic Principles of Harmony, *Choreutics* (the laws of space) and *Eukinetics* (the laws of dynamics). Jooss and Siguard Leeder, during their artistic and pedagogical partnership, gradually systematized and developed these theories. In 1949 Jooss added academic classical ballet to the syllabus, an unprecedented move at the time. Authentic folklore, historical dance forms, jazz and American modern dance were also taught. Jooss saw the dance as a whole; under his leadership there were no competing disciplines. His pedagogical and artistic aims were inseparable.

KEY WORDS Pedagogy, *Choreutics*, *Eukinetics*, Folkwangschule, Rudolf von Laban, Sigurd Leeder.

Early days

Laban said to us in 1920:
You shall see the dance will develop enormously in this century and will be the salvation of mankind.[1]

In the early days nothing could be taken for granted. The new dance evolved through discovery, re-discovery and the need to find a whole natural self, a unity of body and spirit.

From the wish to break away from the overcrusted traditions, forms and behavior, a new natural way of life and also of dancing developed: in the meadows, barefoot, wearing loose skimpy coverings, a sense of unrestricted space, free rhythm on a breath pulse, no music, a tambourine, a gong for a phrase or a crescendo!

"...for the expressionistic dance in Germany in those days, one did not yet need great proficiency; strong intensity was all convincing."[2]

Rudolf von Laban was an enormously stimulating force; his findings, his teachings were a wealth of inspiration to his disciples, some of whom branched out and developed these "principles of movement", these "laws of space", each in their individual way.

Jooss was to become instrumental in developing these findings for the

Figure 1 Folkwangschule, Essen, 1950—Kurt Jooss rehearsing from Labanotation (Photograph by d'Hooghe. Jooss Archives).

professional theatre; when he left the Tanzbɯhne Laban, he   together with his colleague Sigurd Leeder ` investigated and refined Laban's principles more definitively. In 1924 they began to teach, making a clear distinction between recreational dance for everyman and professional dance for the stage.

The same year, after establishing his first company at the theatre in Münster, Jooss became head of the division for movement and dance at the newly opened "Westfälische Schule für Bewegung—Sprache—Musik" (Westfalian School for Movement—Speech—Music).

Subsequently, in search of knowledge of and an understanding of the principles of traditional classical ballet, Jooss and Leeder journeyed to Paris and Vienna.

In 1927 the Folkwangschule, a sequel to the Westfälische Schule was founded in Essen.

Jooss, as co-founder, introduced a dance curriculum which was already quite substantial: Basic Technique[3], Choreutics[3], Eukinetics[3], Dance Improvisation, Composition, Dance Notation, Music, Anatomy, Dance History and other supplementary courses were offered.

The programme also included the "Folkwang-Tanztheater Studio", a creative workshop to develop choreographic abilities and give performance opportunities. The Folkwangschule was unique in 1927 and as such has the oldest tradition today. This "Schule für Ausdruckskunst" (School for expressive art) was a school for Music, Dance and Speech, which also incorporated Theatre, Art History and Criticism. All departments offered professional courses and were run independantly. Interdisciplinary studies were often required and always encouraged, which produced a fertile climate for creative energies.

Movement choirs were an important activity in those days; teachers and movement choir leaders could study and practise at the Folkwangschule with a lively motley crowd!

Finally children's classes were offered as pre-professional training, or for the benefit of the child's general development.

Pedagogical aims and beliefs

Initially Jooss' pedagogical aims and artistic aims were inseperable. He was passionately interested in human beings; individual destiny, contemporary society, and the eternal problems of mankind were his concern and his choreographoc focal point.

He needed to reach out, to touch, to convince and make himself understood through his art—through Choreography. His artistic aims led him towards the development of a new concept of dance, with a new attitude, a new aesthetic and a new technique. This new technique, never codified, was to change with time. Two fundamental principles, however, remained constant: Laban's *Choreutics* (laws of space) and *Eukinetics* (laws of dynamics). The building and tuning of the dance instrument (functional technique) always remained a basic concern, but never without the awareness of *Choreutics* and *Eukinetics*.

In 1928 Jooss already expected every dancer to be a capable theatre dancer, implying that professional dancers must be trained and equipped to serve the needs of the theatre and the independent art of dance.

Jooss' vision for dance in Germany at that time excluded pure classical choreography. He was, therefore, neither concerned with pointe work nor with the virtuosity of classical ballet, but he expected versatile dancers with additional knowledge of various historical and national styles of dance.

Jooss wanted dancers with imagination and scope, able and willing to slip into any role, courtly or rustic, and dance in a repertoire that spanned abstract works, dramatic works and lighthearted comedies. With these aims Jooss began to build his school.

For many years, first in Germany and then in England, the school developed along these lines. The Jooss-Leeder School of Dance in Dartington Hall gradually became known as "the school of the Ballets Jooss" and the dancers of the company were highly acclaimed for their technique and performance qualities.

After the second world war, when Jooss returned to the Folkwangschule, his pedagogical aims had broadened and were far more ambitious. He intended to establish both a Choreo-Gymnasium (for children over 9) and a State Dance Academy (for students professionally concerned with dance). These plans never materialised, but the curriculum of the Folkwangschule was expanded and changed.

It was the beginning of a courageous experiment: Co-equal, daily training in contemporary modern dance and traditional classical ballet (without precedent in 1949!) was introduced. Academic ballet teachers now joined jooss and is faculty to cooperate in this project. Together with the modern syllabus, classical technique, pointe work, pas de deux and classical repertory became part of every student's regular training.

Imported authentic folklore was taught and historical dance forms, researched from dance notation, were studied. Guest teachers for jazz and American modern dance were also invited to supplement the curriculum.

Jooss believed that students would have maximum scope for individual artistic development by studying and absorbing the widest possible range of techniques and styles. Under his leadership, there were to be no competing disciplines; Jooss saw the dance as a whole. He wished graduating students, equipped with a broad education, to have the freedom of choice in their future profession.

Technique

Early Modern Technique: Based on a sense of natural movement, the following fundamental functions were practised:

— Tension and relaxation leading to an understanding of dynamics.
— Awareness of balanced posture and natural breathing.
— Flexibility: stretching, opening and strengthening of all areas of the body.
— Mobility of the pelvis.
— Curling and uncurling of the spine in all directions.
— Rotation: inward and outward rotation of the arms and legs in contrast to parallel, non-rotated gestures and stance.
— Locomotion: various walks, ways of stepping, running, hopping and jumping.
— Turning, spinning, spiraling.
— Balance and off-balance: stable and labile awareness.

Classes began with limbering exercises lying on the floor, or with work in the centre, first in place, then in progression across the floor and down the diagonal. After a general warm up, one or two technical themes were chosen and worked on in different contexts. Exercises frequently evolved spontaneously during the class; these exercises were then often developed into phases and practised over and over again for improvement. In this way one class might be built around the main theme of pelvis circles, leading to weight transfers and jumps, another class perhaps would work on inward and outward rotation leading to turns and circular pathways. The dynamic experience of movement, however, was always of utmost importance; functional technique was never permitted to be an isolated practise.

A loose terminology gradually formed:

eg Impulse	German: Impuls
Body waves	Körperwelle
Scoop circles (gathering)	Schöpfkreise
Strew circles (scattering)	Streukreise
Eight swings	Achterschwünge
Pelvis circles	Hüftkreise
Tilts	Kippungen
Labile turns	Labile Drehungen

It was soon found that practice at the barre was economical and efficient and some modified classical exercises were integrated to supplement the new 'modern' work. Pliés, footwork and all varieties of battments and developés were practiced in combination with torso curls, swings, impulses or labile thrusts, all at the barre. Soon the idea of technical studies evolved; these studies became an integral part of the training method. A study was developed in class over a longer period of time; short sections were worked on and then combined into longer phrases and finally composed into a complete study. Continuity, stamina, dynamic changes and even a degree of dance performance was practised in this way, while working progressively on technique.

The standard of technique rose, bodies changed and the knowledge of anatomical possibilities increased. Their creative imagination led dancers and choreographers on to ceaseless discoveries. The Jooss-Leeder technique has never been given a set syllabus or a formal method. Like Laban, Jooss believed in change, in flexibility and above all in the creativity of the individual.

Choreographic principles of harmony

(Choreographische Harmonielehre)

Laban had been working on a new concept of movement notation for many years. To write, he knew, meant first to analyse. His research led him to Plato and to the Icosahedron[4] which he discovered to be an appropriate structure for the organisation of the Kinesphere[5]. In the Icosahedron Laban found laws of space which enabled the analysis of all forms of human physical action, whether behaviour, work, traditional dance forms or the new, free way of dancing.

The first general term was *Choreographische Harmonielehre*, which Laban soon subdivided into *Choreutics* and *Eukinetics*.

Choreutics: concerned with laws of space and their dramatic content— a theory of space

Eukinetics: concerned with laws of dynamics and their expressive properties —a theory of expression

When Jooss came to Laban, *Choreutics* and *Eukinetics* (then still called *Harmonielehre*) were probably the most exciting new areas for experimentation and discovery.

Later, when Jooss and Leeder began their artistic and pedagogical partnership, they filtered and gradually systematized these theories and developed them for the art of the dance.

Choreutics

Choreutics is a tool for choreographic composition, for meaningfull, communicative movement. The practise of *Choreutics* achieves discipline, co-ordination and sensitivity through awareness of gestural paths (traçe forms) and directional focus through space. An understanding of the contrasting dimensional and diagonal directions stimulates the spacial imagination. Observation shows that there is also an inseparable relationship between human emotion and the direction of spontaneous physical action. A specific emotion will always favour a certain direction or directional path in space.

i.e. If the emotion is sympathy the movement will be forward, conversely the movement will be backward if the emotion is fear.

Joy or hope will always favour high, upward movement, sorrow and hopelessness will be downward.

Choreutics therefore also reveals the psychological content of movement and is thus one of the keys to dramatic dance.

Brief terminology for practical Choreutics

4 fundamental trace forms in any direction:
  Droit, Ouvert, Rond, Tortillé,

6 dimensional directions:
  High, Deep, Side (narrow), Side (wide), Backward, Forward,

3 dimensional planes:[6]
"Flat" (lateral)	= High-Deep, Side-Side,[7]
"Steep" (sagittal)	= High-Deep, Backward-Forward,[8]
"Floating" (horizontal)	= Backward-Forward, Side-Side,[9]

Dimensional scale: sequence of 6 dimensional directions,

Space diagonals: the 4 diagonals of a cube,

Diameters: the 4 diagonals of a dimensional plane,

"The A scale" and "The B scale": two sequences of 12 directions relating to the Icosahedron, alternating "Flat, Steep, Floating."

Eukinetics

Without involving space, no visible action is possible. Therefore an analysis of dynamics must include a spacial element; Jooss named the spacial element Modus.[10]

Time, Intensity and Modus[10] are the basic elements of *Eukinetics*.

1. *TIME*: Quick or Slow, understood as relative properties of speed.
2. *INTENSITY*: Strong or Weak, with much or little muscular strength.
3. *MODUS*: Central or Peripheral, defining the starting point and guidance. ("central movement originates and remains in the centre of the body or the base joint of the limb concerned; peripheral movement originates and remains at the extremities.")[11]

The study of *Eukinetics* begins with experimental improvisation.

Movements can be: 1) Quick or Slow, 2) Strong or Weak, 3) Central or Peripheral. The various combinations of 1, 2, 3, complete the 8 "Eukinetic Qualities"; these qualities are the expressive components of dance. *Eukinetics* is also concerned with sequential flow, with radiating or converging movement and a multitude of dynamic shadings and degrees of change.

Chart of the 8 Eukinetic qualities with the German term:

Time	Intensity	Modus		German term[a]
Slow	Strong	Central	=	Druck
Quick	Strong	Central	=	Stoss
Quick	Strong	Peripheral	=	Schlag
Slow	Strong	Peripheral	=	Zug
Slow	Weak	Central	=	Gleiten
Slow	Weak	Peripheral	=	Schweben
Quick	Weak	Central	=	Schlottern
Quick	Weak	Peripheral	=	Flattern

[a]These German terms were deliberately maintained within the English terminology.

Notes

1. Jooss, Interview 1976.
2. Jooss, Manuscript 1927.
3. See sections: Technique and Choreographic Principles of Harmony.
4. The Icosahedron is the largest regular solid with 20 equilateral triangles and 12 points.
5. The Kinesphere is the space around the human body whose periphery is reachable by extended limbs.
6. Standard terminology in U.S. is: Door plane (lateral); Wheel plane (sagittal); Table plane (horizontal).
7. "Flach".
8. "Steil".
9. "Schwebend".
10. Other names frequently used for Modus: Design, Guidance, Origin, Shape.
11. Ann Hutchinson, Dynamics & Expression, paper 1966.

Choreography and Dance
1993, Vol. 3, Part 2, pp. 53-77
Photocopying permitted by license only

The Dance of Death
Description and analysis of *The Green Table*

Suzanne K. Walther

Kurt Jooss's award winning dance drama *The Green Table* is both a Dance Macabre and an anti war ballet. Its dramatic theme is two fold. The parallel ideas explored in it are man's propensity for violence and his mortality. Violence is indicated through the brutality of war. Mortality is personified in the character of Death. Death is impartial and impersonal, and approaches each of his victims differently according to their own character and personality. The ballet consists of eight scenes. The Prologue also repeated as an Epilogue is a satirical sketch of a conference of power brokers. Each intervening scene is a short dramatic episode in a war where Death is the only victor. The choreography of the ballet is inseparable from its message. Its ideas, events and emotions are communicated directly and entirely through movement.

KEY WORDS   *The Green Table*, Danse Macabre, *Totentanz*, death, war, pacifism.

Introduction

Death is inescapable. It makes no exceptions: rich or poor, genius or simpleton, death takes us all. This idea of death as the great equalizer was the main theme of a bizarre medieval ritual called the Dance of Death. Neither king or peasant could escape this final act, and to the satisfaction of the poor and powerless, all distinctions of status and riches disappeared. To this consoling idea, a moral concept was later added: each person's death was a result of his way of life. Since death was the final act in a series of actions which reflected on a person's character, each person in a way was responsible for the manner of his death.

The Dance of Death originated from a combination of fertility rites, sympathetic magic and miracle plays. The ancient mystery cults of death and resurrection ensured the fertility of the land and conferred immortality on culture heroes. These sources became incorporated into Christianity and Church ritual to form the Dance of Death, or Danse Macabre. It consisted of a fantastic processional through churchyards and cemeteries, led by the figure of Death as a hooded skeleton.

This grotesque ceremony reflected the desperate social and economic conditions of feudalism and the recurrent devastation of the plague. To the poor it was some consolation that wealth and rank did not give protection against the epidemic; for the Church it was an allegory of the frivolity of human vanity. It was a rehearsal for the Last Judgment in which no one can hide from the final verdict. In the midst of devastation, occasionally this ritual took on an aura of defiantly mad gaiety.

Our knowledge of the Dance of Death comes from literature and art. The first representations of it are wall paintings in churches. The earliest are in a medieval church in Klingenthal, Switzerland and in the Church of the Holy Innocents in Paris. There are well-known frescos in churches in Dresden, Lucerne and London, and friezes in Tallin and in the famous Marienkirche in Lubeck. The frieze in the Marienkirche, (which Jooss saw in Lubeck) was destroyed in World War II. In the Lubecker *Totentanz* Death is a skeletal figure wrapped in a white cloth, holding hands and dancing with people from all walks of life. Among the most striking later depictions are the woodcuts of the Dance of Death by Hans Holbein.

Holbein's Death is a quick-footed and agile skeleton. He twists, turns, beats on a tambourine or fights with bone and shield as he takes the Lady, the Nun, the Soldier, the Bishop, and the King and the Queen. Holbein's woodcuts are distinctive for the individuality of each victim. Although they are representative of a class or a profession, each of them expresses personal pain, horror, and grief. Death tirelessly maneuvers each individual into the inevitable final duet—just as he steps forth at the appropriate moment to claim his victim in Jooss's ballet, *The Green Table*.

The inspiration for a ballet has rarely been documented as thoroughly as in the case of *The Green Table*. Jooss told the story of its creation in numerous interviews.[1]

The entire process, from the planting of the first seed in Jooss's imagination to his presentation of the ballet in Paris, took ten years. Of course, he did not work steadily on the ballet for ten years. He toyed repeatedly with the idea of a Dance of Death. Toward the end, when the opportunity came, he nearly refused to choreograph it. His very first inspiration came when he was working with the *Tanzbühne Laban* in Gleschendorf during the summer of 1922. On a visit to the nearby city of Lubeck he was deeply moved by the famous medieval *Totentanz* fresco in the Marienkirche. In an oral history interview he describes his first impression:

I'd seen the famous Lubecker *Totentanz,* a sequence of pictures of all sorts of people dancing with Death who was portrayed as a skeleton. It seems to have been in the medieval period when people's minds were occupied with this kind of dancing, which actually was a symbolic expression for the fact that everyone would die the way he had lived. Death danced with the beggar with the bagpipe, and it was quite nice, an obviously jolly dance. In another picture he danced with a middle-aged peasant woman who had a baby in her arms, obviously dead born, a still-born baby. Probably she also died with this childbirth, and that dance was very gentle in the movement one could see. (Tobias, 1976, pp. 2; 6)

Two years later, while holding the position of "movement regisseur" at the Münster Theatre, he saw *Totentanz* performed by a group of actors who took the motif from those same Lubecker wall paintings. Again the theme impressed him.

In 1926, while on tour with Leeder, Jooss made his first attempt at creating a Dance of Death. His plan was to dance Death first with a scythe; then he and Leeder would alternate, wearing a series of masks, each representing a different character dancing a duet with an invisible Death. Leeder completed eight masks for the project but the dance was never choreographed because of Jooss's incapacitating knee injury.[2]

Another source of a movement idea was a character in the 1930 production of

XXXV

THE NEW-MARRIED LADY

XV

THE ABBESS

XL

THE SOLDIER

XI

THE QUEEN

Figure 1 *Holbein's Dance of Death* originally published in Lyons in 1538.

Georg Keiser's play *Europa* at the *Düsseldorfer Schauspielhaus* where Jooss worked at that time. Keiser was one of the most inventive Expressionist playwrights of the time. The director's idea was to use slides to portray the metamorphosis in which Zeus turns into an angry bull. Jooss was invited in as a guest artist for the role of Zeus and volunteered to dance the transformation scene instead of using the slides. He did it with great success. F.A. Cohen composed and conducted the music for the production. Jooss remembers:

That was in 1930. Anyway, my friend Fritz Cohen, my wife and I worked every evening on that bull. Once on the way home I said to Aino (Siimola): "I must make a ballet where I can be such a beast, it's wonderful. I would like to work on the idea." I forgot about it, but in the end the bull became the way to the figure of Death in *The Green Table*. Together with that I also had the gentlemen in black around this table. That had come as counteraction to the bull which, later on, transferred itself into *The Green Table*. (Huxley, 1982, p. 8)

The Green Table is more than just a Dance of Death. It adds to that the idea of the destructive forces of war. War is the arena where Death becomes the ultimate winner. This second idea was inspired by the terrible experiences of World War One and the ominous shadow that National Socialism cast on Germany by the 1930's. Jooss had become alarmed at the danger of another war from his avid reading of Carl von Ossietsky's leftist periodical *Die Weltbühne*. The main contributor was Kurt Tucholsky; he was exposing the German military's secret rearmament and warning of preparations for a new war.

At the end of 1931, Jooss was asked to enter the choreographic competition at the *Les Archives Internationales de la Danse*. Jooss's initial conception for the ballet was centered around an evil figure, the god Mammon, emerging from a box-like table around which the gentlemen in black, the bankers, play out their drama. Their feuding liberates an evil, destructive force. (Huxley, 1982, p. 9) He changed the entire concept during the six weeks it took him to complete the entire work. In *The Green Table* it is Death rather than Mammon who is unleashed by the gentlemen in black, to preside triumphantly over the war events which are the consequence of their actions.

In an interview with Walter Terry, Jooss talks of the cooperation with composer F.A. Cohen during those six weeks with wonder: "He improvised like magic. We worked like one person on it; we could never account for it" (Terry, 1967, Phonotape).

As the *Folkwang Tanzbühne* was en route to Paris for the competition, Jooss remembers saying "I feel very clearly, this piece will be a tremendous success or an unheard-of theatrical scandal" (Huxley, 1982, p. 10). It proved to be the former, of course. Jooss remembers that the performance:

was incredible. They nearly clapped through the whole piece, which was dreadful, but of course we liked it because it showed us that we had succeeded. (Huxley, 1982, p. 10)

When asked about Laban's reaction, Jooss said: "He was one of the judges. He cried. He was overjoyed" (Huxley, 1982, p. 10).

The competition was held from the second to the fourth of July, 1932. Jooss's ballet was eleventh on the program of twenty works, the fourth out of six pieces performed on July third. The announcement in French read:

THÉATRE DES CHAMPS-ÉLYSÉES

15, AVENUE MONTAIGNE   Téléphone : Élysées 72-43

le 2, 3 et 4 juillet, en soirée

TROIS GRANDES ÉPREUVES INTERNATIONALES DE DANSES ARTISTIQUES

Fondées et Organisées par

LES ARCHIVES INTERNATIONALES DE LA DANSE (A. I. D.)

Sous le Contrôle d'un JURY OFFICIEL

GRAND CONCOURS INTERNATIONAL DE CHORÉGRAPHIE

PREMIER PRIX : 25.000 Frs   DEUXIÈME PRIX : 10.000 Frs

CONCOURS DES PETITS SUJETS DE DANSE

Le 3 Juillet en Matinée

Figure 2 Program notes for the 1932 choreographic competition where *The Green Table* premiered and won first prize.

THÉATRE DES CHAMPS-ÉLYSÉES

15, AVENUE MONTAIGNE   Téléphone : Élysées 72-43

du 2 au 4 juillet 1932 à 20 heures précises

TROIS ¡GRANDES ÉPREUVES INTERNATIONALES DE DANSES ARTISTIQUES

Fondées et Organisées par

LES ARCHIVES INTERNATIONALES DE LA DANSE (A. I. D.)

Sous le Contrôle d'un JURY OFFICIEL

GRAND CONCOURS INTERNATIONAL DE CHORÉGRAPHIE

PREMIER PRIX : 25.000 Frs   DEUXIÈME PRIX : 10.000 Frs

AU PROGRAMME

2 Juillet

Le Ballet Pierre CONTÉ (France)
" LéGENDE ", Ballet de Pierre Conté. Musique de Debussy, Borodine et Ravel. Décors et costumes de L. Clédon. Chorégraphie de Pierre Conté.

Le Groupe HELLERAU-LAXENBURG (Autriche)
" LES CONTRASTES ", Musique de Händel et Prokofieff. Chorégraphie de Rosalie Chladek. Costumes d'Emmy Ferand.

Le Ballet Caird LESLIE (États-Unis)
"APPOLLON ET DAPHNE ", Musique de J. Ph. Rameau. Costumes de Hubert Landau. Chorégraphie de Caird Leslie.

Le Groupe Irena PRUSICKA (Pologne)
" LE SOURIRE DE POLICHINELLE ", Musique de Debussy, Schumann, etc. Chorégraphie d'Iréna Prusicka.

Le Ballet Boris KNIASEFF (Russie)
" LA LEGENDE DU BOULEAU ", Ballet de Boris Kniaseff. Musique de Konstantinoff. Décors et costumes de Mireille Hunebelle. Chorégraphie de Boris Kniaseff.

Le Ballet Dorothée GUNTHER (Allemagne)
" MINIATURES " Suite en 5 danses. Musique de Gunhild Keetman. Chorégraphie et costume de Maja Lex.

Le Ballet Anna KERRE (Lettonie)
" REVERIE ", Ballet d'Anna Kerré. Musique de Chopin, etc. Chorégraphie d'Anna Kerré.

3 Juillet

Le Ballet L. EGOROVA
" LA FLAMME " (dédié à la mémoire d'Anna Pavlova). Livret et musique de Miriam Jaumeton Epstein. Chorégraphie de L. Egorova. Décors et costumes de Mireille Hunebelle.

Le Groupe Jarmila KROSCHLOVA (Tchécoslovaquie)
" L'APRÈS-MIDI D'UN JOUR D'ETÉ ", Musique de Vaclav Smetacek. Costumes de Boska Nevole-ova. Chorégraphie de J. Kroschlova.

Le Groupe Tacyanna WYSOCKA (Pologne)
"IMAGES POLONAISES", livret de Léon Schiller, Musique de Jan Maklakiewiez. Chorégraphie de Tacjanna Wysocka. Costumes de Zofja Stryjenska et Wincenty Drabik.

Figure 2 Program notes for the 1932 choreographic competition where *The Green Table* premiered and won first prize.

La troupe FOLKWANGTANZBÜHNE DE LA VILLE D'ESSEN (Allem.)
" LA TABLE VERTE " Danse macabre de Kurt Jooss. Musique de F. A. Cohen. Chorégraphie de Kurt Jooss. Costumes de Hein Heckroth.

Le Ballet Janine SOLANE (France)
" L'ABANDON CELESTE ", Ballet de Janine Solane. Musique de Richard Wagner. Chorégraphie et costumes de Janine Solane.

La Troupe Pino MLAKAR (Yougoslavie)
" UN AMOUR DU MOYEN AGE ", Ballet de Pia Mlakar. Musique de Vivaldi, Händel, Bach. Chorégraphie de Pino Mlakar. Costumes de Wilhelm Reinking.

4 Juillet

Le Ballet Astrid MALMBORG (Suède)
" RHAPSODY IN BLUE ", Musique de George Gershwin: Chorégraphie d'Astrid Malmborg. Décors et costumes de Sandro Malmquist.

Le Ballet Ursel RENATE HIRT (Allemagne)
" LA FEMME D'AUTRES CIEUX ", Ballet d'Ursel Renate Hirt. Musique d'Edouard Künneke. Chorégraphie d'Ursel Renate Hirt. Costumes de R. Göpfert.

Le Groupe TRUDY SCHOOP (Suisse)
" FRIDOLIN EN ROUTE ", Pantomime comique de Trudy Schoop. Musique arrangée par T. Kosics et W. Kruse. Costumes de Hermann Leisinger.

Le Ballet Tony GREGORY (France)
" DANS LA RUE ", Ballet dansé et mimé de Tony Grégory. Musique de Lennox Berkeley. Chorégraphie de Tony Grégory. Masques de Raymond Gid.

Les Ballets Triadiques du prof. Oscar SCHLEMMER (Allemagne)
Musique : " Baroque Allemand ", suite d'après les maîtres anciens de A. Pachernegg. Chorégraphie d'Oscar Schlemmer. Costumes du professeur Oscar Schlemmer.

Le Groupe Gertrude BODENWIESER (Autriche)
" LES HEURES SOLENNELLES ", Livret et chorégraphie de Gertrude Bodenwieser. Musique de Tchérépnine et de Mayer-Lorber. Costumes de Lizzi Pisk.

Le Ballet Lidya NESTEROVSKAYA (Russe)
" LE SOUFFLE DU PRINTEMPS ", Musique de Chopin, Glazounoff et Strauss. Chorégraphie de Lidia Nesterovskaya. Costumes de Mme Ivanova.

Chacune de ces troupes ne paraîtra qu'une seule fois et les résultats seront proclamés
LE 4 JUILLET EN FIN DE SOIRÉE

Les concurrents seront présentés au public par
M. DESSONNES, Secrétaire de la Comédie Française

Chefs d'Orchestre : MM. T. Kosics, E. Künneke, V. Smetacek et E. Bigot

Pour ces représentations exceptionnelles le **Prix des Places** est de **100 fr. à 10 fr.**

Le 3 Juillet, Matinée à 14 h. 15
CONCOURS DES PETITS SUJETS DE DANSE
Epreuves définitives pour sujets admis et hors-concours

" LES ENFANTS "
Ballet de Magd. Bouchorit - Le Faure, réglé par ROBERT QUINAULT

Prix des Places, de 50 à 10 frs.

Figure 2 Continued.

La troupe FOLKWANGTANZBUHNE DE LA VILLE D'ESSEN (Allem.) "LA TABLE VERTE"
Danse macabre de Kurt Jooss. Musique de F.A. Cohen. Choregraphie de Kurt Jooss. Costumes
de Hein Heckroth.

Immediately after the competition Jooss went on tour with the ballet. He
counted close to 4000 performances before he stopped counting (Terry, 1967,
Phonotape). Since its creation *The Green Table* has never been out of repertory. It
was premiered in America by the Ballets Jooss at the Forest Theatre in New York
City on October 31, 1933 with Jooss as Death. People who saw him remember it
as an extraordinary performance.

In 1967 the Joffrey Ballet became the first American company to produce *The
Green Table*. Since then several companies have performed it both nationwide and
worldwide. The synposis of the ballet is as follows:

THE GREEN TABLE

BOOK AND CHOREOGRAPHY: Kurt Jooss

MUSIC: F.A. Cohen
      (For Two Pianos)

COSTUMES: Hein Heckroth

PREMIERE: July 3, 1932

ORIGINAL CAST:

Death	Kurt Jooss
The Standard Bearer	Ernst Uthoff
The Young Soldier	Walter Wurg
The Old Soldier	Rudolf Pescht
The Young Girl	Lisa Czobel
The Woman	Elsa Kahl
The Old Mother	Frida Holst
The Profiteer	Karl Bergeest

The Gentlemen in Black, The Soldiers, The Women:

Lola Botka, Frida Holst, Elsa Kahl,

Lucie Lenzner, Masha Lidolt,

Hertha Lorenz, Trude Pohl

Karl Bergeest, Rudolf Pescht,

Heinz Rosen, Ernst Uthoff, Peter Wolff,

Walter Wurg, Hans Züllig

Order of Scenes:

1. The Gentlemen in Black
2. The Farewells
3. The Battle
4. The Refugees
5. The Partisan
6. The Brothel
7. The Aftermath
8. The Gentlemen in Black

Duration: 35 minutes.

SCENARIO:

Prologue—The Gentlemen in Black

The curtain rises following a few powerful, ominous measured chords of musical introduction. The music softens to a sarcastically pleasant little tango. On the two sides of a long rectangular green table are positioned ten elderly gentlemen. The table looks like a felt-top conference table. It is foreshortened and slopes upward toward the back: the audience perceives it as flat, yet its whole surface is visible. The men are in tuxedos and white gloves. Each wears a mask with exaggerated features. With one exception they are exceedingly bald with longish fringes of gray, red or dark scraggly hair. Their foreheads are high and bumpy, their expressions are supercilious. Some have drooping mustaches and one has a long gray beard. They are obvious caricatures but they take themselves deadly seriously. They are the power brokers, and they are in deep disagreement. Each side of the table represents a faction.

At first their debate preserves the veneer of civilized behavior. There is no discernible right or wrong side; the opposing forces are exactly equal in number and demeanor. They spy on each other's conversation, or pretend to be uninterested. Slowly shedding the mannerisms of upbringing, they lose their tempers and begin to slap the table. Insincerity oozes from every gesture.

The essence of this conference is that nobody means what he says and nobody says what he means. Realizing at last that agreement is out of the question, they line up at the front of the stage. As if on command each draws a small revolver from his breast pocket. For a moment the two factions threaten each other with revolvers aimed. But then, in ultimate solidarity with their kind, they face the audience and simultaneously discharge their revolvers into the air. The stage goes dark. War has been declared, but others will do the fighting.

Invisible in the dark, men and table vanish as a rumbling rolling piano chord is played. Then, in front of the black curtains which frame the entire stage area, the figure of Death becomes visible. He is a combination of soldier and skeleton. Black leather straps outline his rib cage and pad his shoulders like protruding joints. The bones of his legs and arms show black on his light gray colored costume. A black leather shield on his hips is a skeletal reminder of pelvic bone. His face is skull-like, eyes black sockets, nose and cheeks hollow. On his head a military helmet is made taller by a large coxcomb. Loose-topped midcalf boots echo the shape of coxcomb and pelvic shield. He is large, self-assured and arrogant. A gladiator in the guise of a skeleton, he brutally plunges into a powerful solo.

Death here is an incarnation who knows his time has come, his time to rule as a warrior. He moves to an insistent beat which is a musical evocation of the underworld. Death has been conjured up and given free rein. He proudly pulls himself up to his full height. Briefly extending his arms to the sides, he takes the position of a cross projecting his power to the four corners of the world. Insistently but methodically he begins to mobilize his forces. He beats endless time with his feet as he raises and lowers his fists. The flow of time itself is an act of his will and a manifestation of his invincible power.

The Farewells

To the insistent timeless beat of Death, the troops sign up for battle. First to arrive is the Standard Bearer. He gestures forcefully with a white flag that cleaves the air with sharp snapping reports. His uniform consists of a silver helmet, gray tights and a white harness across his chest: a stylized version of a uniform from The Great War. He marches proudly and the music takes on heroic tones. He is joined by three soldiers in similar outfits, eager, enthusiastic, moving vigorously, training with imaginary bayonets and swearing allegiance to the glorious flag.

Next comes the Young Soldier followed by the Young Girl. She does not want him to go, but he joins the other soldiers on the march as she slowly pulls away. Meanwhile a trio, the Old Soldier, his Old Mother and a woman arrive. Again the farewells are painful, but duty calls and he joins his comrades as the woman and the mother comfort each other. The two younger women wear plain mid-calf length dresses with short sleeves, one in pale yellow and the other in flaming red. The Mother wears a full-length brown dress with long sleeves covering her arms and a gray bonnet tied under her chin. The younger ones' heads are wrapped in tightly rolled head scarves.

Suddenly the Profiteer enters. He is dressed in black tights and white T-shirt, white gloves on his hands, white spats on his feet: bowler hat in hand he salutes the crowd. As the soldiers begin to move he starts clapping, urging on the procession. As they march into battle with imaginary bayonets drawn, Death looms large in front of them. He stands with outstretched arms, under which the soldiers pass on their way to battle. The Woman in red, after a moment's doubt, resolutely joins them. She becomes The Partisan, thereby deciding her own fate.

The Profiteer notices the prostrate figure of the Young Girl, and sweepes down over her like a large bird of prey. With a slight turn of his torso, Death acknowledges his first victory. Everyone there has passed into his realm.

The Battle

On the battlefield the fight rages around the flag. It has lost its pristine whiteness and bears traces of blood and mud. In hand-to-hand combat bodies are punched, shoved, beaten, and slashed with imaginary weapons. The flag, a sacred symbol for which blood flows, is always in sight. The two sides, equal, dressed alike and looking alike, attempt to keep or to take possession of the flag. In orderly and repetitious battle, the participants group and re-group. It is a brutal but predictable scene: formations engage in combat; the wounded and dying fall; the living urge each other on.

Suddenly, unexpectedly, as if emerging from a whirlwind, Death appears, rising to his full height in center stage. In his left fist he grips the wrist of a dying soldier. He lets go contemptuously, without looking, an easy victory, and the soldier falls to the ground. The battle field is strewn with corpses. Death begins his first victory march. High-stepping and pompous, he is a dark knight, detached and powerful, leaving a well-accomplished work on the battle field.

He hardly exists before agitated chords signal the arrival of The Profiteer. Catlike, he wends his way among the corpses looking for opportunity. With delight he spots a ring, probably a gold wedding band. He slips it from the dead finger and examines it, turning it this way and that. Perhaps sensing that he has strayed too close to the wake of Death, he runs leaps over the corpse he has just plundered and rushes off.

The Refugees

A slow sad ballad accompanies a slow-moving group of women led by the Old Mother and including the Young Girl. Fearful, hugging, helping each other, they travel on strange terrain. Surveying the unknown, the Old Mother is afraid, but resigned; to her it doesn't matter any more. Moving to a voice that only she can hear, she is caught in an ever-narrowing circle. The music luring her on has a sweet tone, it is almost a lullaby. Then a harsh chord is struck and the light shows Death, crouched in wait, beginning to rise. The refugee women freeze in their tracks and stare at the rising figure with horror. The Old Mother is supported by The Young Girl as the others run. Death lifts his arms invitingly but with clenched fists that regally affirm his will.

Slumped in the arms of The Young Girl, the Old Mother listens to Death calling. She makes a feeble attempt to flee, but Death extends his arms in an invitation. The Mother moves in a trance toward Death. He takes her outstretched hand and leads her in a courtly dance. Then suddenly he points out the unmistakable way to the end. When she is resigned to go he picks her up, gently cradling her like a child in his arms, and carries her out impassively.

Once again, as Death leaves, The Profiteer appears. This time it is the Young Girl, prostrate with grief, who attracts his attention. Lacking the strength to escape him, she lets herself be led away.

The Partisan

Eloquently heroic and uplifting chords herald the arrival of The Partisan Woman. Holding a long pale yellow scarf in outstretched arms above her head, she leaps high off the ground in long strides, circles around and signals with the scarf like a semaphore. She whips it from side to side, a symbol of liberation and of the homemade, makeshift weaponry of guerrillas and revolutionaries everywhere. Tucking her weapon into her belt, she undertakes her brave but hopeless mission. Though committed and passionate, she must still conquer her moments of doubt and fear. She gathers her strength, rising to ever greater heights of fervor and self-sacrifice.

She scouts the area, lying low on the ground as the first line of troops arrives. These are not the vigorous enthusiastic soldiers we saw in battle. These are battle-weary heavy-footed troops on a long march. The Partisan reconnoiters, her resolve building. As the second line of soldiers moves by she pursues them, catching up to the last soldier in the line and flicking her scarf around his neck. As he falls to the ground, Death steps out behind him, arms out in the powerful position of the cross. Simultaneously three soldiers appear and train their guns on The Partisan. Death folds his arms and begins to move toward her. She sees the soldiers and Death approaching; an invisible string pulls her to the execution ground. With great deliberation Death steps behind her, lifts his arms, and in a staccato movement signals the firing squad to kill.

The Brothel

Prostitutes and soldiers sway in hurried sensuality to a jazzy waltz. The Young Girl, procured by The Profiteer, stands alone, frightened. The Profiteer shows her off to his customers; he claps his hands and forces her to pay attention. Fearfully and reluctantly, she accepts the first soldier, who grabs her and rushes her through a brutal duet. The next soldier approaches savagely and pulls her into another merciless duet. A third follows; she crumples to the floor. The Profiteer signals the company to leave and offers The Young Girl to the last waiting soldier. He pulls her up and they engage in a semi-tender duet, his lust tempered by her battered fragility and his need for momentary human companionship. In this instant of vulnerability Death steps in to take the place of her last lover. He pulls her into a final sadistic high-stepping dance, driving her mercilessly until she willingly steps into his arms seeking rest. He bends over her in a final carnal embrace, then stares at the audience, insatiable.

The Aftermath

Death, crouched behind the Old Soldier and shadowing his movements, takes the flag from him effortlessly and the two of them begin the processional. All of the dead join in, forming a long row: The Old Soldier holding on to Death's arm, followed by the Partisan Woman, The Old Mother, The Young Soldier, The Young Girl, more soldiers. They march in a circle, frozen in the postures characteristic of their manner of death. Death in the middle is holding up the flag tainted with blood and dirt; they all march to his rhythm now. At Death's command the dead slump to the floor and lie still. At this moment The Standard Bearer enters as he had earlier. His inspiring music and enthusiasm are quickly withered by the stare of Death, and he joins the ghastly procession as it leaves the scene.

Now the Profiteer enters, on his last prowl. He also senses danger and looks searchingly for its source. Suddenly he finds himself face to face with Death. Death advances in large powerful strides and The Profiteer backs away, trying to escape. But it is too late; he is already caught in Death's sphere, no matter how he twists, turns and scurries about. Death ignores The Profiteer: a minor irritant, a cockroach on its last run. While preparing for his final victory solo, Death sweeps up the wriggling Profiteer.

All have died. Death has accomplished his task, and dances to celebrate his power. The war has given him a wonderful feast, but he remains implacable, insatiable, ever ready for his awesome task. With an unexpected movement he disappears as swiftly as he had appeared.

Epilogue—The Gentlemen in Black

The lighting comes up to reveal The Gentlemen in Black exactly as we had left them. We hear again the shot fired simultaneously from their pistols, and see them still standing in a row. Tucking their pistols back into their breast pockets, they file back to the table and take up the exact positions they held at the beginning. Again the argument takes place in exactly the same gestures, with one difference: this time their movements create no sound. When they bang on the table we cannot hear it: the fake drama is now even further from reality. Visually the action and the world are the same, but the experience of Death has distanced us so that we now see it *sub specie aeternitatis*.

The theme

In 1976 Jooss made the following statement: I am firmly convinced that art should never be political, that art should not dream of altering people's convictions.... I don't think any war will be shorter or avoided by sending audiences into *The Green Table*. (PBS Television, 1982)

Despite Jooss's disclaimer, the ballet is considered a monument to pacifism. But *The Green Table* is not political propaganda. It does not exhort, instruct or coerce; it does not label or pass value judgments; it does not take sides. Jooss presents a series of dramatic events from which the audience must draw its conclusions. Notwithstanding Jooss's apolitical stand, *The Green Table* evoked political associations from the very beginning. Jooss mentions some of the early interpretations:

it was always brought into some kind of relationship to current politics. For instance, when in our first Paris season, in May 1933, all of a sudden, in the applause, they started to shout at us: "A Lausanne, á Lausanne, á Lausanne, á Lausanne!" In Lausanne was the disarmament conference which was completely idle and had gone nowhere. And then, there was always the mistake that people thought the table scenes were the League of Nations. I never meant the

League of Nations. I couldn't have meant the League of Nations, because the war scenes were obviously scenes from the First World War. The table scene, however, had to be before the war and at that time there was no League of Nations. I didn't mean anything specific. I meant that which one doesn't know, but which somehow exists, these powers which are just to be felt and not seen. (Huxley, 1982, p. 10)

The topic of the ballet is as timely now as it was at its creation. Even when threatened by global annihilation, men continue to fight wars.

The Green Table has two main themes: its treatment of death and its anti-war message. To anthropomorphise, to give human qualities to the forces of nature, is a characteristic of human thinking. When death is given a human form, even if it be a skeleton, this is an attempt to understand the essentially incomprehensible, our own mortality. The successful personification of Death is one of the most significant elements of *The Green Table*. Awesome in appearance, a combination of heraldic knight, soldier and skeleton, Death provides the connecting thread of the story.

With the pistol shot of the prologue, Death has received a special mandate. Since war is now declared, he appears as a soldier. The job which he ordinarily does quietly and discreetly in bedrooms and hospital rooms can now be done publicly with fanfare. Man has played into his hand, making his job easy. He has no need to find and stalk his prey: it comes to him of its own accord. His appearance brings a chill into the air. He is bathed in a greenish light, his skeletal features immobile. With him comes a temporary suspension of the ordinary rules of existence. The duration of war is an extraordinary time, a time of natural disaster. Death is almost a natural force like an earthquake or a storm. Once let loose it gathers momentum and subsides only after spending its fury.

Since War lets loose the forces of destruction, the ideas of War and Death are inextricably intertwined. War provides the arena in which Death performs. The forces of evil lie not in Death itself, but in the power brokers at the conference table who let Death reap an untimely and rich harvest. Death himself is fearsome but impartial; he only collects what is duly his. Each person's fate has been decided and the mode of his death is a consequence of his own way of life. Death adapts himself to every circumstance.

Death has no disguise but many faces. They appear in his manner of treating each of his victims. He is cold, hard and merciless with the armies who massacre each other, making his task absurdly easy. As a superior warrior he steps into their midst and suddenly the battlefield is strewn with corpses. He is firm but courtly toward the Old Mother, compelling in his call but gentle in his approach. As if captain of the firing squad, he gives the signal to shoot when the Partisan is executed. He is rough but sensuous with the Young Girl, and she finds peace in his final lover's embrace. He is impatient with the Profiteer, who does not realize that he and his victims are caught up in the same web. He tries to escape and dies cringing in fright, devoid of all dignity. Death does not have to fight for the lives of these people. Each character is doomed, and as Death wills them to die the will each merges with his.

The dramatic treatment

Dramatically each character is larger than life, representative not only of a type but of a whole class of people. Critic Allen Storey wrote that in Jooss's ballets:

figures become units, soldiers become armies, brothels turn into nations where mental prostitution is rife and intelligence is dulled with craving for pleasure. (Storey, 1940, p. 596)

The Old Mother represents all mothers who suffer losses in a war, and all the old and feeble who have come to the end of their road and accept the call of death. The Young Girl is all women brutalized by men, for whom death offers welcome relief. The soldiers represent all the armies of the world, mobilized with visions of glory and ending up dead on the battlefield, their ideals as soiled as their flags. The Profiteer stands for all those who take advantage of other people's misery and think they can get away with it: those who fish in muddy waters and welcome disaster, cleverly turning it to their advantage. The Gentleman in Black are symbolic of the special interests of power, greed, prejudice, intolerance and the various ideologies, all those petty prides and jealousies which turn nation against nation and cause the suffering and devastation of war.

The dramatic format—A B C B A, in which A = Prologue and Epilogue, B = solos by Death—gives a cyclical character to the ballet. After his last solo Death suddenly disappears, but we know that he has not gone far. He is only hibernating, waiting for man to give him his next opportunity to take charge openly again.

There is a striking contrast between the tone of the Prologue and Epilogue and the intervening episodes of the ballet. This deliberate difference serves to highlight the events following the exchange at the conference table. The Prologue and Epilogue are satirical, painting a wicked caricature of the power brokers. Self-important, supercilious and calculating, each character casts a comic but frightening figure.

From the first moment, a constant communication is occurring around the table. They are real human beings, not puppets as is often stated. They are anonymous but their masks are designed to exaggerate individual characteristics. They are engaged in a conversation of global importance. Their decisions will affect the lives of millions, yet they remain devious and deceitful. They show off the imaginary medals on their chests, and engage in heated arguments. They throw up their hands in dismay, insist on a point with raised finger, nod or shake their heads, listening, lecturing or clapping. The gesture is the essence of the choreography here; it is through their stylized gesturing that we understand the motivation of these characters.

Five Gentlemen are "sitting" at each side of the table. Actually they are squatting in a pose which simulates sitting. The tableau comes alive as each person simultaneously turns to his neighbor with his arms raised: questioning and explaining, incredulous and argumentative. As they turn back, the last Gentleman on the right stands up and shakes his raised arms, palms open, in an impatient gesture: "Gentlemen, don't you understand?!" This gesture occurs several times and it always stands out clearly, a warning or perhaps an admonition. Similarly, the "philosopher", an old man with a long white beard,

Figure 3 The Gentlemen in Black from *The Green Table* (Photo: Renger-Patzsch, 1932, Jooss Archives).

repeatedly poses with a pointed finger: an important idea! He is pompous, self-important and sarcastic as he mockingly claps at intervals.

The "dreamer" is right front: his elbow rests on the table and he stares into space. An accusing finger is thrust toward him from the opposite side. When this opponent is moved to action he puts an outstretched leg insolently on the table, or jumps on top of it and shakes his fists. They all periodically slap the table with open palms. The Gentleman on the left rear cups a hand to his ear trying to overhear his opponents' private conversations. In a highly ingenious movement they all lean horizontally on the table and with lowered foreheads push toward each other. This gesture feigns deference with a bow, while suggesting an aggressive bull-like readiness to lock horns. Straightening, they tilt backward proudly or sway back and forth. Sometimes one side tilts forward and the other backward like a see-saw. These variations are quite comical, but they keep increasing the agitated mood around the table. At one point, using the table for support, they all push off, piercing the air in back with their legs.

As the argument gets heated they march away from the table, hands clasped in fists. They return with a gesture, palms up then down, "maybe yes, maybe no." As they lobby in small groups each faces an opponent. They slice the air with chopping gestures, count on their fingers, or shake their palms in a gesture of "No!" When no agreement is reached they walk around agitated, torso bent parallel to the ground as if wisdom or solutions could be found there. Frustrated and furious, they take up fencing positions and thrust and parry. Quickly realizing the folly of this action, they bow to their opponents. Then with a mechanically bouncing little toe-heel step, one hand tucked into the lapel and the other swinging by the side, all return to their original positions at the table. Some of the initial movement sequences are repeated with additional leaps onto the table.

Having failed to reach an agreement they begin to move in unison with military precision and purpose. The factions form up in two separate lines at the front of the stage. Swiftly and elegantly they pluck small revolvers from their breast pockets. Facing each other they crouch and aim for a moment threatening each other. In an instant they realize the possible consequences, bow low with the sweep of an arm, face outward, and fire into the air. Let others do their dirty work.

The covert aggression and overt politeness of the Gentlemen in Black keeps the tension at a high level. Their gestures exhibit their calculating and deceptive nature; they pontificate, threaten, swagger and spy. They are inflexible but agile in jockeying for advantage. The tone echoes the gravity of the situation. Its mood turns more severe as tempers rise. The last chords turn into a menacing drum roll that foreshadows the arrival of Death.

There is a stunning contrast between the comic figures and facile gestures of the Gentlemen in Black and the stark appearance and commanding motions of Death. We are plunged from light to dark, from a realm of playful if sinister sophistication to one of brutal and deadly realities.

Death rises from a wide deep knee bend, shifting his weight and straddling space, pulling himself up from the underworld, his arms gathering strength from the earth. As he reaches his full height he begins to move, his arms wielding his characteristic trademark, the scythe. Leaning slightly and shifting his weight, he raises this imaginary scythe and brings it down with closed fists. He cuts through space, slashing the air on a plane in front of himself with open palms. All the while his feet are stomping in a steady six-beat pulse. Concentrated in this sweeping movement is a devastating show of power and purpose.

Death moves proudly as he cocks his head, tilts backward like a rearing horse, and thrusts a knee out in front. At the same time he raises one clenched fist above his head, holding the other in front of his body. He has risen on the ball of one foot and for a second he holds this pose, his outline etched in space. Then with a quick change of direction he pierces the air with a swift backward kick and slices the space above it with a horizontal chop of the hand. With arms raised he grabs at the sky on both sides of his body; bringing them down he gathers in the space in front of him. The world belongs to him and there are no limits to his power. He leaps into the air with a turn; landing on the diagonal he thrusts with his arms as if he were wielding a sword. Then with one arm sweeping above his head he again projects his power over the whole of space, as if encircling it with a rope or capturing it in a net.

In this forceful solo, using only a few precisely crafted movement combinations, Death conjures up the images of horseman, coachman, swordsman and grim reaper: all the imagery associated with death since the Middle Ages. His steady, rhythmic stomp marks the passage of time, his greatest weapon. The scope of his power is made palpable by the dynamics of his movement and its mastery of the surrounding space. The solo is accompanied by an eerie, insistent drum roll on the pianos and the heavy staccato echoes of his stomping feet.

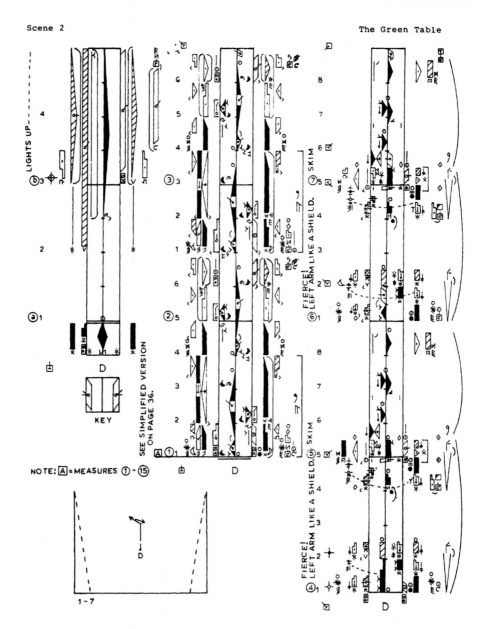

Figure 4 *The Green Table* Death's opening solo or the 'A' theme. Notated by Gretchen Schumacher, revisions by Jane Marriett, dynamic and verbal annotation by Odette Blum.

Our first image of Death is as a brutal destructive force. But Death proves to be as versatile as the diverse ways of dying; he presents a new face in each situation. He calls the armies to war, endowing them with his own physical power. Marching in place, he rhythmically flexes and relaxes his biceps, ratcheting his forearms up and down. The ingenious combination of six steps in place achieves the double effect of a marching soldier and a figure eternally marking time.

In each episode Death appears suddenly, always at the climax the moment when his time and consequently his victim's time has come. At the end of the battle scene he rises up out of a whirlwind of fighting and dying soldiers. He stands tall and strong among the wounded, his arms extended to the sides, fists clenched. The dying raise an imploring arm before expiring. He then surveys the scene like a general on his high-stepping horse, pulling in his reins. He is both horse and horseman in this brutally elegant movement.

With the Old Mother he plays the Knight. He turns to her in a compelling calling gesture, one arm held high and one extended toward her, palms invitingly opened, three fingers extended in unholy benediction. He ritualistically holds two extended fingers up as in a church ceremony. He lowers himself to one knee in front of her and she bows to him in reverence. Stepping behind her with a cavalier bounce in his step, hands on his right hip where the hilt of a sword would be, he leads her in a few measured steps and she follows graciously. Then like a semaphore he tilts, pointing the way she has to take with a compelling motion of his hand. She turns away once more in horror, then gives in to his will and settles herself in his arms. Unrelenting but knightly, he slowly walks away cradling The Old Mother's dead body.

With The Partisan Woman, Death is as relentless as the fate which she chose when she decided to kill. His arms hug his own body and then lift upward in front as if he is folding himself in an imaginary cape. Then he turns to stand behind her as the soldiers line up to form the firing squad. She opens her arms wide; Death raises his folded arms above his head. As she is shot he opens hs arms into the cross position as she slowly turns and falls at his feet. Death places two hands on a hip and lifts his head in triumph.

He is most expansive with the Young Girl, as if he relished the role of seducer. As her final human partner approaches her we see Death dogging his steps. The man steps blindly past her—having slipped into the realm of death, she is invisible to him—and it is Death who takes her outstretched hands. With large powerful strides Death begins his seduction as brutally as the soldiers in the brothel. He grabs her by the buttocks and pulls her tightly to him. After a few steps in this vulgar embrace he takes her hand and makes her run around him in a large circle. His right arm is swinging above his head as if he were wielding a whip, and he skips in place, literally driving the Young Girl to her destruction. After this pitiless recapitulation of her humiliation by the men before him, he wraps her in a tender final embrace, offering solace as her savior. He rocks her gently to the floor and bends low over her prone figure, sensuous and victorious in his double conquest.

From the Old Soldier Death takes away the flag and with it his life. The Old Soldier might have not realized that the war is over, and keeps hanging on to the flag protective. But Death appears behind him, grabs the flag and with it the soul of the old soldier. The Standard Bearer feels the cold breath of death in a moment when in a few remembered movements he tries to recapitulate his glory. His life fades away as did his glory and he becomes one of the puppet like corpses in the final procession.

The last one to die is the Profiteer. He jumps on stage with outstretched arms, landing like a big bird of prey, at the very moment when Death arrives to perform his final victory dance. The Profiteer is the opposite of Death in every way. While Death stands tall, erect and imposing, the Profiteer bends low and crouches furtively. His body is coiled and curved; he springs like a cat and slithers like a snake. While Death moves in a heavy staccato and angular manner, the Profiteer hops and skips, moving through space as if it were a medium lighter than that which ordinary mortals occupy. He is a mercurial wheeler-dealer, a sociopath, thief, pimp and coward.

In the brothel he pushes and shoves the Young Girl into the embrace of the lecherous soldiers. Playing the host, he claps for attention as he manipulates his women into the arms of his clientele; then he rubs his hands together in delight at the success of his establishment. Spreading his palms, he shows off his merchandise like a satisfied businessman. As he leaves the Young Girl alone with the soldier who bought her he exits backward, scraping and bowing in deference to the only power he knows: profit.

When the time comes for him to die, the Profiteer uses all his ingenuity attempting to escape. He traverses the stage with a remarkable series of forward and backward steps, curious and fearful, shielding his eyes with his hand as he peers about. When he sees Death approaching he shrinks back in horror. He ducks down into a crouch and tries to elude him by shifting directions. Death pays no attention to him, and plunges into the initial movements of his first solo. What was then a recruiting march is now a victory dance. As it becomes more heated and savage the Profiteer becomes desperate. He lunges and runs but can't escape. Death now holds him on an invisible string. The Profiteer hurls himself to the floor repeatedly, his legs shoot upward as his face is pressed into the ground. Death sweeps him up without missing a beat. The Profiteer rolls out in a somersault like a clump of weed carried off by the wind.

The world in which Death has collected his dues is defined by war. Everyone is a war victim. The women have lost sons, husbands or lovers. One joins the Partisans, one falls prey to a pimp, and many become refugees. The Old Mother, leader of the refugee women, walks before them with small steps, fearful but resigned for she has little left to lose. She is supported by the Young Girl who would have been her daughter-in-law in time of peace. Her body is bent and she looks frail, one arm hanging from a crooked elbow like the broken wing of a bird. She clasps her hands in prayer, then peers ahead shielding her eyes. Looking into the future and afraid of what she has seen, she shrinks back and finds refuge in memory. With rocking steps she pats the air with her hands, like the top of a remembered child's head. Her arms move in soft large circles; then as reality intrudes she claws at the air and runs in concentric circles like an animal in a cage. When Death beckons she lifts a hand to her ear: she hears his call and she knows it is meant for her. Supported in deep knee bend her body sags head down in complete resignation. Lifting an arm she begins her slow approach to him.

The Partisan is all courage and determination. She shoots across space in a straight line, her hands holding a scarf stretched tight above her head. The scarf takes on the characteristics of a weapon. She turns, signals, coils her body tightly and drops low to the ground, ready to attack. Her movements alternate between the tightly stretched line, ready to snap with tension, and the spiraling curve which coils and uncoils, gathering strength and fury. She is searching for the enemy, and her upward stretching jumps and low crouches evoke the mountainous territory where guerrilla warfare is usually fought. She flattens close to the ground as the soldiers march by her, then springs up, leaping, circling, slashing out, gathering force like a tornado, then unleashing her weapon at the best target, the last of a column of tired soldiers. Her mission accomplished, she accepts capture and the firing squad with open-armed resignation. The soldiers who pull the trigger lower their head in silent homage to this courageous woman.

The Young Girl is a passive victim of male exploitation. She stands in her simple yellow frock, her kerchief discarded and her hair flowing freely. Her hands are protectively wrapped around her body. The Profiteer brings her to attention and forcefully propels her forward. She is defenseless as one soldier after another picks her up, tosses her and spins her around. She lunges in repeated attempts to escape from this brutality. Totally exhausted, she lies down to rest, but is quickly pulled to her feet again. Rest will come only at the end, with Death. The degrading effect of war is seen in the fact that the brave soldiers who swore allegiance to the flag with idealistic fervor are now brutalizing a defenseless woman in a brothel.

The Standard Bearer is the epitome of heroic leadership. As the soldiers assemble, his silver helmet gleams and his flag slashes through space in inspired circles and planes. The spring in his heroic step marks the same beat as Death's stationary march. Both are calling up the troops: one to win, one to die. The Standard Bearer embodies all the idealistic illusions of youth: the symbolism of the flag, the shining uniforms, the masculine glory of the fight. He will also be the last soldier to die.

The scene entitled The Aftermath is a superb moment for Death. Taking possession of the bedgraggled, dirty, blood-splattered flag he leads all his victims in a slow processional, each of them frozen in his most characteristic pose. The Old Soldier hangs lifelessly to his arm, one hand held up swearing eternal fidelity to the flag. After him comes the Partisan, her hands clasped on her chest as they were just before she opened them wide at the moment of her execution. The Old Mother holds a hand to her ear, perpetually listening to the call of death. After her comes a soldier from the firing squad, holding his arms ready to pull the trigger. He is followed by the Young Girl, her arms open, her head and body bent to the side in eternal exhaustion. The soldier who was killed by the Partisan is in the posture of a hanged man, a reminder that he was choked to death. This lamentable group files past with slow halting steps as Death holds the flag aloft with both arms.

Now Death stands in the center and commands the proceedings. The dead revolve in a circle around Death, moving forward and backward with small puppet-like steps. Death is like a soldier hampered by stiff armor: with mechanical motions he triumphantly lifts and lowers the flag. The dead form a semicircle in front of him and he draws the flag over them in an arc. Like dominoes they crumple to the floor and lie stretched out, as if finally in their graves. Death lowers the flag to the ground like a spear, his legs spread wide and his left hand on his hip.

At this point the Standard Bearer enters. He moves with the same fervor as before, but Death lifts a hand and he falters, his body jerking in convulsive

Figure 5   Kurt Jooss rehearsing the role of Death in *The Green Table*, Wuppertal, 1974 (Photo: Borzik, Jooss Archives).

contractions. Several times he tries to go on, but Death thrusts with the flag and the Standard Bearer crumples. He joins the ghastly army, the ever-lengthening line of the dead. Once more Death leads this procession across the stage, holding the flag high in the solemn and tragic march which celebrates his victory.

The statement and the message

The Green Table is a statement on the senseless brutality of war. It demonstrates that war, regardless of its motivating forces, causes damage, destruction and untimely death. The main ideas of the ballet are as valid today as they were at its creation. Jooss choreographed the ballet between two World Wars. He believed that preparations were again being made for war in the name of peace, in spite of the horrors of the first World War. *The Green Table* is a cautionary tale. Episode by episode, it documents the unrelieved horror of war.

The great irony of war is that it is said to be necessary for the sake of a better life and a safer world, yet it threatens the very existence of both. Premature death, undue suffering, and the brutalization of the spirit are the actual result of war: The world has not become a better place when the Gentlemen in Black reassemble at the conference table at the end of the ballet. Their arguments are resumed exactly where they left off. On the other hand, perhaps the eerie silence of their movements during the Epilogue suggests that we have moved beyond history into a shadow world where Man eternally plays out his compulsive power games. *The Green Table* is a pacifist ballet based on humanitarian principles.

The two parallel themes of *The Green Table* cut to the core of man's existence: his violence and his mortality. Jooss paints a cutting, satirical picture of the abuse of power. It becomes clear from the manner of the participants at the conference table that grave consequences flow not only from gross abuses but from small insincerities, advantage-seeking and manipulative behavior as well. The Gentle men in Black make crude threats in moments of anger when the veneer etiquette wears thin, but they quickly recover themselves. They d personally engage in the barbarity of war, but what they unleash upon is the very beast that glared out of their faces in their unguard

Jooss's impartiality is more damning than any apportionmr be. The evil cannot be assigned to an army or a cause. It lie irrational ways of thinking, fanaticism, greed and aggression. The p. of Death which the ballet depicts emerges whenever men make war, regarai. the reasons and rationalizations which may be given.

Death is also a normal part of human existence, of course. It is curious that we think of death as separate from us, a visitation from the outside at the end of our life. In reality we carry death within ourselves from the moment we are born, but we cleverly conceal this from ourselves. The ballet's personification of death gives shape and character to our amorphous notions. This terrifying half-knight and half-skeleton, the elegant mythical monster figure of Death, is a composite of our fearful imaginings.

Nevertheless, Jooss shows us how an individual's own personal character affects his own death. Not that life and death are predictable, as if no horrible accident or disease could fell us. Absurdity is as characteristic of death as it is of life, but the capricious side of existence offers less provocative material for artistic and philosophical contemplation. There is validity in the old saying that he who lives by the sword, dies by the sword. Personal decisions shape our lives, our deaths and the fate of those around us. With Jooss a focus on the individual is always a commentary on society as well.

Each person has within himself the potential to live responsibly and to die with dignity. Death seen as apart from us is a part of us as well. At the end his will merges with ours, the presumed duality disappears, and Death becomes one with fate.

Notes

1. The interviews referred to here were conducted by Tobi Tobias, John Gruen and Walter Terry. The interview with Michael Huxley was conducted as a part of a doctoral research project at the University of Leeds, England. A transcript appeared in *Ballett International* on the fiftieth anniversary of the ballet's premier. (Huxley, 1982, pp. 8-12)
2. Photographs of the masks exist and are printed in A.V. Coton, *The New Ballet*, p. 88.

Selected Bibliography

Huxley, M. The Green Table, a dance of death: Kurt Jooss in an interview with Michael Huxley. *Ballett International*, August-September 1982, pp. 8-12.

Figure 6   *The Green Table* Rudolf Pescht in the role of the Old Soldier and Kurt Jooss in the role of Death (Photo: Lipnitzki, 1932, Jooss Archives).

Tobias, T. *Interview with Kurt Jooss*. Transcript of tape recording, September 26, 1976. Oral history project of the Dance Collection of The New York Public Library at Lincoln Center.
Terry, W. *Interview with Kurt Jooss*. Phonotape, 1967. Dance Collection of the New York Public Library at Lincoln Center.
Storey, A. The art of Kurt Jooss. *The Dancing Times*, July 1940, pp. 546-597.

Choreography and Dance
1993, Vol 3, Part 2, pp. 79-91
Photocopying permitted by license only

Dancing for Jooss
Recreating the role of Death in *The Green Table*

Christian Holder

The following essay relates the author's personal experiences with the choreographer Kurt Jooss over a ten year span. The focus of these experiences is the recreation of the role of Death in the ballet *The Green Table*, during the 60's and 70's while the author was a member of The Joffrey Ballet. Included are anecdotes regarding the intensive personal instruction and coaching of the author by Mr. Jooss in the rehearsal studio and on stage.

   Also mentioned is the author's work experience with Mr. Jooss' daughter, Anna Markard, who now carries on her father's work, and has invited the author to appear as guest artist in subsequent productions of *The Green Table* in Europe and America.

KEY WORDS   The Joffrey Ballet, Anna Markard, Maximiliano Zomosa, Ernst Uthoff, Ingmar Bergman, The Seventh Seal.

Maximiliano Zomosa and The Joffrey

My first meeting with Kurt Jooss was heralded by weeks of anxiety and serious pangs of insecurity. It was early in 1970, and we, the Joffrey Ballet, were

Christian Holder (Photo: Roy Round)

preparing for our spring season in New York. Jooss had supervised the final rehearsals of the company's original production of *The Green Table* when it was first mounted in 1967, and he felt it necessary to return now because of our upcoming London debut. English audiences had been well acquainted with *The Green Table* since the nineteen thirties, when Jooss and his company made their home base at Dartington Hall, Devon, and performed across the country and Allied Europe. Furthermore, several dancers had left Joffrey since Jooss had last seen the company, and he felt it was time to take a look at the new crop of performers who were interpreting his work.

By this time, I had already been dancing the role of Death for the better part of a year, and my graduation from being one of the Gentlemen in Black to portraying the ballet's central figure had been a dramatic one. At the age of nineteen I had been catapulted into the formidable position of having to follow Maximiliano Zomosa's definitive interpretation of Death. Max had, in fact, been grooming me for the part with Joffrey's approval, when it was learnt that he had committed suicide because of what he must have perceived as insurmountable personal and legal entanglements. Thus, I was called upon to replace him in the ballet several months sooner than anticipated.

For two years I had watched Max dance this ballet which he worshiped. His passion for *The Green Table* was immense and all-consuming, and often he appeared to be driven by some supernatural force. He knew every step of every character, and at the end of his coaching sessions with me I would sit rapt as he recounted anecdotes about the first time he ever saw the ballet, and about subsequently working with Jooss. Max had danced the role in Ernst Uthoff's company in Chile, and Joffrey had been so impressed with his performance during the company's 1965 New York visit, that he invited Max to join the newly christened City Center Joffrey Ballet so as to ensure an articulate, secure focal point for the new 1967 production mounted by Mr. Uthoff.

Max's final performance was riveting. He infused his portrayal with more than the usual amount of passion, and then for his solo bow he removed his helmet and set it on the table where the masks of the Gentlemen in Black are placed for the curtain calls. We all assumed that this was just Max being theatrical; but in hindsight this significant gesture of relinquishment urges one to believe that he had already decided that his life should end.

Max then disappeared for a while, with no one volunteering information as to his whereabouts. This was when Joffrey asked me if I were ready to perform the role of Death. Joffrey was always loath to change the programs once they had been submitted, and there was no other dancer available who knew the part. Michael Uthoff, Ernst's son, was a senior member of the company, and should have been next in line, but he was presently the only Standard Bearer we had, so it was not feasible for him to switch characters. Also, Michael's wife, Lisa Bradley, was on maternity leave, and Michael, too, had given in his notice, so Joffrey had already begun to shape the company's future without him. The understanding was that when Max returned I would alternate performances with him. I agreed.

When Max did show up again we were in a rehearsal period in New York in the winter of 1968/69. After one of our coaching sessions he took me aside and told me that he wanted me to have his Green Table boots. I protested, saying that he would need them when we started performing again, and that I had already been fitted for a pair of my own. Max was intransigent, however, and insisted that I

Figure 1 Conductor Seymour Lipkin, Kurt Jooss, and Robert Joffrey watch Marjorie Mussman, and Lisa Bradley during a studio runthrough in 1967 (Photo: James Howell).

Figure 2   Maximiliano Zomosa, Kurt Jooss, and Ernst Uthoff at the Joffrey studios in 1967 (Photo: James Howell).

keep his boots. A couple of days later Joffrey fought back tears as he informed us that Max's body had been found in his car in New Jersey.

Working with Jooss

By nature I tend to be quick, light and supple in my movements, so acquiring the necessary weight and solidity for the role of Death was not an easy task. In addition, Max had personalized his performance to such a degree that it was impossible for me, or our ballet master, to extract from what we had seen an objective base on which to build my own interpretation. My only recourse, I felt, was to attack the choreography with as much ferocity as I could muster. This seemed to work to a certain extent, even though I knew I was far from discovering a true personal identity with the role.

I had not been able to sleep the night before Jooss' scheduled appearance. The ballet's place in the company's repertoire was at stake. What if Jooss didn't approve of my interpretation? What if he decided to withdraw the ballet? Negative scenarios did battle with my strong desire to succeed. I had to make a good impression, not just for myself, but for Joffrey...and for Max.

The man whom Joffrey escorted into the studio the next day assuaged most of my fears instantly by his mere presence. His bearing was gracious and genial, and his soft, white wavy hair made me think instantly of Father Christmas. He greeted the few dancers he had worked with before with a courteous nod of his head, then Joffrey called me over and introduced me. Jooss extended his hand for me to shake, and looked me over with polite, optimistic curiosity. I had seen Mr. Jooss, of course, in 1967, when the company was first introduced to him en masse. However, I had not been called to any of the subsequent rehearsals, so he had no knowledge of my work.

The dancers set up the wooden table in the center of the studio; our pianist played the first ominous chords of Fritz Cohen's score, and the runthrough began.

I knew, when we had finished, that I had done my best. But would that be good enough for Mr. Jooss? He thanked the company for their efforts, then approached me as I stood at attention, my heard pounding from exertion and apprehension. He merely smiled and said pensively, "You dance it very well...but, it's a little wild, hmmm?"

The next few days provided some of the richest moments of my professional life. I spent wonderfully intense hours in the studio with Jooss, then continued my rehearsals with Leonide Massine, who simultaneously was mounting a production of Petrushka for the Joffrey.

Ironically, I found that although the roles of the Blackamoor in Petrushka, and Death are worlds apart, they nevertheless had certain physical aspects in common. Both required a sense of weight which was hard for me to retain consistently, and both employed a solid, square second position plié. Interestingly, I found that working on each character's specific physical challenges helped me with the other's.

One of the first things that Jooss made clear to me in Death's opening solo was that it was not necessary to stamp out the signature combination (or the 'A' theme as it is musically referred to). Noise did not equal strength. This was difficult for me to let go of, because I felt that I was being stripped of one of the few ways I had at my disposal to make a powerful physical statement—Max had made noise very effectively, so I felt that I should do the same. I found, however, that when I related to the floor with the sense of weight and gravity that Jooss instilled in me, I actually felt and looked far stronger than I ever had before. The noise, in fact, was merely incidental.

Jooss spent many an hour with me banishing old preconceptions and refocusing the role's specifics so that it would become honest and valid for me. I was advised not to think of Death as a demonic or evil apparition. Jooss conceived the role, he informed me, as an angel of death, a majestic being who had, by definition, the fate of the entire human population at his fingertips. Vengeance or passionate emotions on a human level did not enter into it. In fact the only figure who inspires contempt from Death is the Profiteer, whom he casts away into oblivion.

We also worked on my focus. This was all important, especially because my face would be hidden beneath the black and white makeup. The opening steps with the "scythe" motif were differentiated so that for the first three counts the gaze was fixed front at a specific target at close range as the arms crossed the body. Then as the arms and the head returned to their upwardly diagonal direction the gaze became "universal', scanning all the way to the back of the auditorium and infinitely beyond, only to surprise the audience once again by reverting inexorably to the front.

The imaginary use of the scythe (the harvesting tool that the figure of Death is sometimes seen carrying in medieval paintings and woodcuts) in these same movements had presented bloodcurdling imagery to Max, who had interpreted the movements as "cutting off their heads and throwing them out to the horizon". When I presented this metaphor to Jooss he smiled inwardly and said, "...Well...Max was always very dramatic. I allowed him certain liberties because he was very theatrical, and they suited him."

Jooss' eyes were large and pale, and I remember the potency of his gaze as he demonstrated how Death should scan the horizon. Omnisciently, yet devoid of any emotion, he would turn his head slowly from side to side with a regal sweep, never blinking, and never deigning to be in the least bit personal or sympathetic.

Figure 3   Christian Holder dancing Death's opening solo (Photo: S. Stroppiana).

He would stand in the middle of the studio, impassive like an old regal lighthouse whose luminous beam (Jooss' eyes) penetrated the dense fog for miles around.

For Jooss, the most imperious image came at the end of the third scene when death strides off the corpse-littered battlefield. "It is as if you are standing, victorious, in a chariot," he explained, "and you have the reins of three white chargers in each hand. Behind you your cloak is billowing in the wind. You are immense... Part the Red Sea!" We worked for most of that rehearsal on the travelling step which is repeated until Death disappears in the downstage right wing. As I suspended my leg in attitude, then shot it down ahead of me and closed my other foot behind in a tight, conclusive fifth position, he would accompany me vocally, "Rrraaah...taaah! Rrraaah...taaah!"

The focus at the end of the Partisan's scene was then clarified. After giving the order for the three soldiers to execute the passionate woman in red, Death's port de bras appears to have him sheathe an imaginary sword at his left hip. He then turns his head to look over his shoulder with supercilious defiance. Max had instructed me to look straight out to the back of the house at eye level, which gave the moment a confrontational, human coloring, as if Death were 'speaking' to the audience. Jooss preferred a more remote attitude here. He accomplished this by having me change the level of my gaze, so that as I turned, I looked upward to the balcony. In fact, in performance I looked directly into the spotlight as it pinpointed me on the darkened stage, while simultaneously lengthening my spine and pressing down my shoulders. This, Jooss felt, gave this intimate moment an aloof quality which was still awesome, yet kept Death's reaction elevated above mere human sentiment. Joffrey, however, had Max's image firmly ensconced in his memory, and he coaxed persistently after Jooss' departure to have me revert to the old way of acting out the scene. Eventually I compromised by looking at first directly out into the house, then raising my head to the balcony just before the spotlight faded out.

For me, the most touching example of Jooss' artistry came when he demonstrated the relationship of Death to the character of the Old Mother. Death is portrayed in this vignette as a galant cavalier who materialises in order to rescue the exhausted woman from her unending journey as one of a group of refugees. Jooss acted out both roles for me alternately with a sensitivity and subtlety that inspired tears. He often had trouble with his right knee which would not always support him, but this gave his motions a frailty and caution which, as the Mother, added to the eloquence of his portrayal. In addition, his age (he was sixty nine) and experience, endowed his every gesture with a sense of space, time, and knowledge that was riveting in its simplicity.

For the Mother, Death's appearance causes her to recall the romance of her youth; perhaps in her fantasy she remembers a favorite beau. As she responds to Death's command, all her apprehension and fear leave her, and she shares a moment of gentle nostalgia with her partner. Abruptly, Death is given a lunging gesture here that clearly indicates the inevitability of the woman's fate. She shrinks from this rude awakening but then silently obeys and is carried off like an infant in Death's arms. All these subtle changes in demeanor were a constant challenge for me. Here, especially, there was the temptation to show emotion. Jooss emphasised that Death in this instance should merely be courteous. He could also be accomodating and indulgent to a point, but ultimately there should be the same unswerving sense of mission to his character.

Death's appearance in the Brothel scene which follows also has abrupt changes of character. He enters as the shadow of the Young Girl's final assailant, and dances with her hungrily as did the rough, boisterous soldiers earlier on. Finally, he opens his arms to the girl who runs to him as if he were a paternal saviour. Jooss reminded me here that all these various transitions are seen through the girl's eyes, and that Death only mirrors the way in which she, or any of his captors, has lived. After having been violated by the indifferent customers at the brothel, the girl is thrown together with the Old Soldier by the Profiteer. Could it be that the girl's father was the same age as this war veteran? Perhaps the Old Soldier has a daughter who resembles the hapless waif now at his disposal. Whatever subtext one might find to motivate these two sensitive characters in this scene, they do share a brief, poignant moment of mutual understanding before the girl is rocked to sleep in Death's arms, and gently laid to rest as he then crouches protectively over her. Here, Max had given this haunting tableau a menacing attitude which conjured up the image of a lion glancing up from his prey. Jooss accepted this approach with reservations, but went on to say that Death need not be insatiably animalistic, he need only raise his head as he guards his lifeless ward. His work has been done. There is choreographically no need to then comment further on the situation.

While working on the next section of the ballet, The Aftermath, Jooss related to me the story of the time when his Ballets Jooss were on tour in England in 1945. He remembered that he was dancing the role of Death, and that as he plucked the ravaged flag from the hands of the Old Soldier and started to triumphantly lead all his assorted victims across the stage in bleak profusion, the sound of church bells began to echo through the theatre: peace had been declared—World War II was over. Jooss' eyes twinkled as he remembered what must obviously have been a rich, pungent experience.

Jooss explained that in The Aftermath the Old Soldier is valiantly holding fort, unaware that the fighting has ended. He senses a presence behind him, but only glimpses his fate for an instant before Death wrests the tattered flag from his grip. The ensuing image of Death leading his conquests in a dance can be found in many medieval works of art. It was at this point in our work together that Jooss suggested that I view the Ingmar Bergman film The Seventh Seal, and indeed it proved to be for me the most valuable piece of homework. Mr. Bergman had presented brilliantly a foreboding, enigmatic spectre of Death playing chess with a knight from the Middle Ages. More importantly, at the film's climax there was the chilling silhouette of Death leading all those whom he had taken in a meandering dance atop a barren, craggy hill. How interesting, I thought, to ascertain whether Ingmar Bergman had seen Jooss' ballet which had been created some twenty or so years prior to this film.

The ensuing confrontation with the Profiteer is simply and effectively wrought by Jooss, and is the perfect liaison to bring the ballet full circle to a reprise of Death's opening solo. Death's focus as he enters is again far out onto the horizon, head and shoulders above the retreating Profiteer. Jooss has given Death a long diagonal path to establish a sense of infinity, then once he reaches center stage, his repetitious, piston-like steps bring to mind the magnified pulse of a heart, a life force. The choreography has the upper and lower body counterpointing each other to a musical phrase of five. The legs pursue an even staccato rhythm, while the upper body contracts and expands in a more legato fashion, with accents on the fourth counts of the first four bars, and then on the first counts of the next four bars. The dancer here should employ his entire back and arm span to give the illusion of reaching across the stage from wing to wing, and up from the floor to the 'flies'. The eyes remain inexorably focused on the horizon straight ahead. All these elements when executed with precision and power establish a sense of steadfastness which acts as an effective foil against the syncopations of the fugitive Profiteer as he alternately runs from, then attacks the figure of Death. It is only when Death decides that he has tired of this wretched being who has dared to challenge him that there is a moment of eye contact between them. Then the Profiteer is hurled away with disgust.

Finally, the reprise of the triumphant opening solo before the return of the Gentlemen in Black at the table, reestablishes the inevitability of Death's presence. The difficulty at this stage of the performance is that no matter how intense and powerful one might have been up to this point, one now has to surpass all that the audience has seen. They have witnessed the same steps when the solo is first danced some twenty five minutes earlier, so this time around there is absolutely no room for faltering, or for allowing fatigue to have the upper hand.

My first performances after working with Jooss were challenging indeed. Across the United States Joffrey audiences had become used to Max's furious interpretation, and then, subsequently, mine. Now I had to make them believe this new creation which in many ways was more subtle than before. Generally, I think I can say that I succeeded.

Jooss arrived in London in time for our première at the Coliseum Theatre. He seemed pleased by our efforts, although he noticed immediately everything that had been altered by Joffrey in his absence. During our stage rehearsal we could hear him whispering notes and corrections into his pocket sized tape recorder. He thanked us over the intercom after the first performance was over, and left the following day. I'm not sure, though, how satisfied he actually was. There is never enough time in the theatre, especially when a complete repertoire has to be rehearsed within a limited amount of stage time.

In 1975 I was lucky once again to have the opportunity to work with Mr. Jooss. This time we worked on the *Big City*, a cautionary tale of a ballet told deftly with skillful economy. I wanted desperately to dance the role of the jaded Libertine who ruins an impressionable young girl's life. Jooss, after much reflection, however, felt that my being black would in this instance throw an unintentionally racial context on the ballet. I understood, but was nevertheless disappointed. Still, I was chosen to lead the hedonistic Charleston section which was great fun to dance. The Charleston, performed by the ballet's cynical upper class characters, was masterfully juxtaposed with the working class couples' Bal Musette. This Jooss accomplished by having the respective dancing couples "fade" in and out almost cinematically, as their musical themes wove a subtly discordant counterpoint. Once again, Jooss used only lighting and a simple black velour curtain to create potent images that lasted in the mind's eye long after the ballet had ended. It was theatre in its simplest yet most effective form.

Later that year PBS' Dance In America television series featured *The Green Table* and other Joffrey repertory staples in an hour long presentation. Although we only danced the first two scenes from the ballet, it nevertheless afforded me the opportunity to work once again with Jooss. By this time we had developed a

Figure 4   Kurt Jooss instructs Christian Holder at a rehearsal for the Dance In America television program in 1975 (Photo: Herbert Migdoll).

rapport beyond that of teacher and student. He was interested in my background, and asked which roles gave me the most satisfaction as a performer. He spoke about José Limón (whose role I danced in The Moor's Pavane), and about German dance pioneers Mary Wigman and Harold Kreutzberg, and recounted humorous anecdotes about working with the exotic dilettante Ida Rubinstein in Paris.

The following year Joffrey succeeded in persuading Jooss to revive the complete "Jooss Evening" consisting of *Big City*, *Pavane On The Death Of An Infanta*, *A Ball In Old Vienna*, and *The Green Table*. The short, potent evening, which was interspersed with evocative piano interludes, was a resounding success; much, I suspect, to Jooss' surprise. He was a humble man, and quite critical of his own works, and I suspect that at heart he was slightly unsure as to how these ballets would be accepted by contemporary American audiences. He need not have worried. Although some critics observed that the ballets were dated in the sense that they were obviously of another era, still they could not argue with the craft and theatricality of these early creations.

It was around this time that Anna Markard, Jooss' daughter, began working with us. She was already dedicated to preserving her father's work, and immediately set about resolving any ambiguities in the choreography. Being a creative artist, Jooss was often tempted to adapt elements of his works if he felt the dancer he was coaching was worthy of it. In fact, he had embelished a few gestures for me because of my stature, and the fact that I had different things to offer the role which he had originally created for himself. Anna's point of view was that the choreography should remain unchanged, and that dancers should adapt to it rather than the other way around. This was actually very good for me because it forced me to broaden my capabilities.

Jooss' legacy to me

It was during the first week of June in 1979 that I heard a rumour that Jooss had died. I was devastated. We were at the Opera House in San Francisco, half way through our annual summer tour, when a few company members got news from home that an announcement regarding Kurt Jooss had been made on various news broadcasts. No one, however, seemed completely sure of the details. When Massine had died, Joffrey had called a company meeting to inform us. He hadn't uttered a word about Jooss; in fact, we hadn't even seen him for a day or two. I couldn't stand not knowing, so I called Patricia Barnes (at that time married to dance critic Clive Barnes) in New York. She confirmed the sad news, telling me that Jooss had indeed died from injuries sustained in a car accident over a week before!

On the following day I urged Trinette Singleton, a company member, and one of Joffrey's assistants, to have Joffrey change the program that night so that we could perform *The Green Table*. He agreed, and I made an announcement at the end of the intermission just before the ballet, dedicating the impromtu performance to Kurt Jooss' memory.

It was an intense, heartfelt performance in which the atmosphere both on stage and out front was thick and electric. The audience gave us a standing ovation, and we all gathered together after the final bow to shed tears of love and dismay. Several of us had shared a long history with Jooss. For me it had been just short of ten years; ten years during which time I had learned volumes about stage craft and character development, gesture, and the ability to hold an audience's attention when merely standing still. All of these aspects of the dance had been garnered while working with, and watching, Kurt Jooss.

When I left the Joffrey a couple of months later, I lamented the fact that I would probably not have the opportunity to dance the role of Death again. Happily I was wrong. Ms. Markard, being appreciative of my dancing and my dedication to *The Green Table*, has invited me to appear as guest artist in productions in Finland, Italy, and Germany, as well as here in the United States. Thus, to date, my last performance of this masterpiece was in 1985 in Essen, Germany, where it was created. Should I be given the opportunity to dance this ballet once more I would, naturally, leap at the opportunity. If not, I feel grateful and proud to have been able to interpret the role of Death over a span of

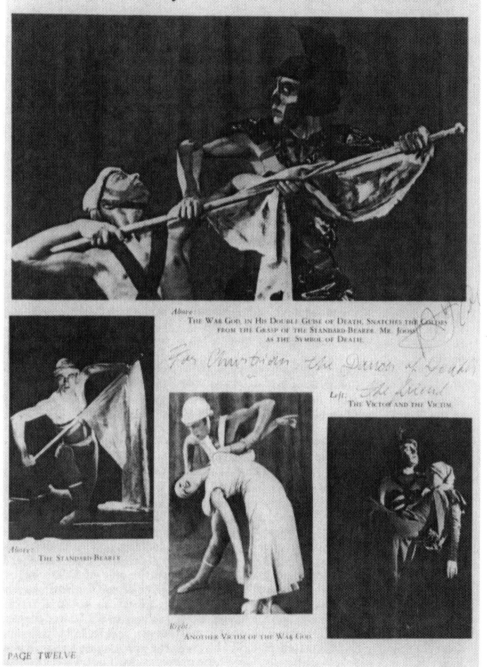

Figure 5   Autographed page of the 1933 American concert appearance souvenir program.

seventeen years. Working with Papa Jooss (as he liked to be called) has enriched me as a performer and as a choreographer. He was a great humanitarian, a gentleman and a gentle man of the first order.

One day in 1975, while new camera positions and angles were being discussed by the technicians on the Dance In America set, I asked Papa Jooss if he would be kind enough to sign a souvenir program that I had obtained from a 1933 American concert appearance. His eyes glistened as he reminisced fondly about that New York engagement forty two years before. He turned to the center pages of the program where there were several photographs of him as Death, thought for a few seconds, and then wrote, "For Christian, the Dancer of Death, the friend." I feel greatly honored.

Choreography and Dance
1993, Vol. 3, Part 2, pp. 93–102
Photocopying permitted by license only

Jooss Ballets
Chronological list

1924	Persisches Ballet Tanz-Suite
1925	Der Dämon Die Brautfahrt Groteske Larven
1926	Tragödie Kaschemme
1928	Seltsammes Septett
1929	Drosselbart Zimmer Nr. 13 Suite 1929 Pavane auf den Tod einer Infantin/Pavane on the Death of an Infanta
1930	Petrouchka Gaukelei Le Bal Polowetzer Tänze
1931	Copélia Die Geschichte vom Soldaten Der verlorene Sohn/The Prodigal Son
1932	Pulcinella Der Grüne Tisch/The Green Table Grosstadt von Heute/Big City Ein Ball in Alt-Wien/A Ball in Old Vienna
1933	Seven Heroes/Die sieben Schwaben The Prodigal Son/Der Verlorene Sohn
1934	Persephone

1935	Big City/Grosstadt Ballade The Mirror/Der Spiegel Johann Strauss, Tonight!
1937	Seven Heroes/Die sieben Schwaben
1939	A Spring Tale/Die Brautfahrt Chronica The Prodigal Son/Der verlorne Sohn
1943	Company at the Manor
1944	Pandora
1948	Juventud
1951	Dithyrambus Colombinade
1952	Weg im Nebel/Journey in the Fog Nachtzug/Night Train
1955	Persephone
1956	Der verlorene Sohn/The Prodigal Son Catulli Carmina
1959	Die Feenkönigin/The Fairy Queen
1962	Castor und Pollux
1964	Persephone
1965	Der Nachmittag eines Fauns/Afternoon of a Faun
1966	Phasen/Phases Dido und Äneas/Epilog
1969	Rappresentazione di anima e di corpo
1972	Belsazar Acis und Galathea

Alphabetical list

When titles are given in two languages, the original title is listed first, but the alphabetical ordering is determined by the English title.

Acis und Galathea
  Music: Georg Friedrich Händel
  Design: Veniero Colosanti/John Moore
  Date: 1972
  Place: Salzburg Festspiele, Germany
  Under the Direction of: Herbert Graf

Der Nachmittag eines Fauns/Afternoon of a Faun
 Music: Claude Debussy
 Design: Hermann Markard
 Date: March 8, 1965
 Place: Leverkusen
 Company: Folkwangballett

Le Bal
 Music: Vittorio Rieti
 Design: Hein Heckroth
 Date: November 1930
 Place: Opera House, Essen, Germany
 Company: Folkwang Tanzbühne Essen

A Ball in Old Vienna/Ein Ball in Alt-Wien
 Libretto: Kurt Jooss
 Music: Joseph Lanner (arranged by Fritz A. Cohen)
 Design: Aino Siimola
 Date: November 21, 1932
 Place: Opera House, Köln, Germany
 Company: Folkwang Tanzbühne, Essen, Germany

Ballade
 Libretto: Kurt Jooss
 Music: John Coleman
 Design: Hein Heckroth
 Date: September 23, 1935
 Place: Opera House, Manchester, England
 Company: Ballets Jooss

Belsazar
 Music: Georg Friedrich Händel
 Design: Veniero Colosanti/John Moore
 Date: March 1972
 Place: Grand Theatre, Geneva, Switzerland
 Under the Direction of: Herbert Graf

Grosstadt von Heute/Big City
 Libretto: Kurt Jooss
 Music: Alexandre Tansman
 Design: Hein Heckroth
 Date: November 21, 1932
 Place: Opera House, Köln, Germany
 Company: Folkwang Tanzbühne Essen

Big City/Grosstadt
 Libretto: Kurt Jooss
 Music: Alexandre Tansman
 Design: Hein Heckroth
 Date: 1935
 Place: Dartington Hall, Dartington, England
 Company: Ballets Jooss

Castor und Pollux
Music: Jean-Philippe Rameau
Design: Jean-Pierre Ponnelle
Date: 1962
Place: Schwetzinger Festspiele, Opera House, Essen, Germany
Under the Direction of: Erich Schumacher

Catulli Carmina
Music: Carl Orff
Design: Dominik Hartmann
Date: October 22, 1956
Place: Opera House, Düsseldorf, Germany

Chronica
Libretto: Kurt Jooss
Music: Berthold Goldschmidt
Design: Dimitri Bouchène
Date: February 14, 1939
Place: Arts Theatre, Cambridge, England
Company: Ballets Jooss

Colombinade
Libretto: Kurt Jooss
Music: Johann Strauss/Aleida Montijn
Design: Rochus Gliese
Date: 1951
Place: Opera House, Essen, Germany
Company: Folkwang Tanztheater/Ballets Jooss

Company at the Manor
Libretto: Kurt Jooss
Music: Ludwig van Beethoven
Design: Doris Zinkeisen
Date: February 15, 1943
Place: Arts Theatre, Cambridge, England
Company: Balletts Jooss

Coppélia
Music: Leo Delibes
Design: Hein Heckroth
Date: February 25, 1931
Place: Opera House, Essen, Germany
Company: Folkwang Tanzbühne Essen

Der Dämon
Music: Paul Hindemith
Design: Hein Heckroth
Date: March 1925
Place: Municipal Theater, Münster, Germany
Company: Neue Tanzbühne

Dido und Äneas/Epilog
  Libretto: Kurt Jooss
  Music: Henry Purcell
  Design: Ekkehard Grübler
  Date: 1966
  Place: Schwetzinger Festspiele, Opera House, Essen Germany
  Under the Direction of: Erich Schumacher

Dithyrambus
  Libretto: Kurt Jooss
  Music: Georg Friedrich Händel
  Design: Dimitri Bouchène
  Date: 1951
  Place: Opera House, Essen, Germany
  Company: Folkwang Tanztheatre/Ballets Jooss

Drosselbart
  Libretto: Kurt Jooss
  Music: Wolfgang Amadeus Mozart
  Design: Hein Heckroth
  Date: March 1929
  Place: Opera House, Essen, Germany
  Company: Folkwang-Tanztheater-Studio

Die Feenkönigin/The Fairy Queen
  Music: Henry Purcell
  Design: Jean-Pierre Ponelle
  Date: 1959
  Place: Schwetzinger Festspiele, Opera House, Essen, Germany
  Under the Direction of: Erich Schumacher

Gaukelei
  Music: Fritz A. Cohen
  Design: Hermann Haerdtlein
  Date: May 2, 1930
  Place: Opera House, Essen, Germany
  Company: Folkwang-Tanztheater-Studio

Die Geschichte vom Soldaten
  Music: Igor Stravinsky
  Design: Hein Heckroth
  Date: 1931
  Place: Opera House, Essen, Germany
  Company: Folkwang Tanzbühne Essen

Der Grüne Tisch/The Green Table
  Libretto: Kurt Jooss
  Music: Fritz A. Cohen
  Design: Hein Heckroth
  Date: July 3, 1932
  Place: Théâtre des Champs-Elysées, Paris, France
  Company: Folkwang Tanzbühne Essen

Groteske
  Libretto: Kurt Jooss
  Design: Hein Heckroth
  Date: 1925
  Place: Municipal Theater, Münster, Germany
  Company: Neue Tanzbühne

Johann Strauss, Tonight!
  Libretto: Kurt Jooss
  Music: Johann Strauss (arranged by Fritz A. Cohen)
  Design: Georg Krista
  Date: October 21, 1935
  Place: Gaiety Theatre, London, England
  Company: Ballets Jooss

Weg im Nebel/Journey in the Fog 1952
  Libretto: Kurt Jooss
  Music: Adeida Montijn
  Design: Robert Pudlich
  Date: 1952
  Place: Opera House, Essen, Germany
  Company: Folkwang Tanztheater/Ballets Jooss

Juventud
  Libretto: Kurt Jooss
  Music: Georg Friedrich Händel
  Design: Dimitri Bouchène
  Date: 1948
  Place: Santiago de Chile
  Company: Ballet del Instituto Musical

Kaschemme
  Libretto: Kurt Jooss
  Music: Fritz A. Cohen
  Design: Hein Heckroth
  Date: October 1926
  Place: Municipal Theatre, Münster, Germany
  Company: Neue Tanzbühne

Larven
  Libretto: Kurt Jooss
  Music: Kurt Jooss (Schlagzeug)
  Design: Sigurd Leeder
  Date: October, 1925
  Place: Municipal Theater, Münster, Germany
  Company: Neue Tanzbühne

The Mirror/Der Spiegel
　Libretto: Kurt Jooss
　Music: Fritz A. Cohen
　Design: Hein Heckroth
　Date: September 28, 1935
　Place: Opera House, Manchester, England
　Company: Ballets Jooss

Nachtzug/Night Train
　Music: Alexandre Tansman
　Design: Robert Pudlich
　Date: 1952
　Place: Opera House, Essen, Germany
　Company: Folkwang Tanztheater/Ballets Jooss

Pandora
　Libretto: Kurt Jooss
　Music: Roberto Gerhard
　Design: Hein Heckroth
　Date: January 26, 1944
　Place: Arts Theatre, Cambridge, England
　Company: Ballets Jooss

Pavane auf den Tod einer Infantin/Pavane on the Death of an Infanta
　Libretto: Kurt Jooss
　Music: Maurice Ravel
　Design: Sigurd Leeder
　Date: October 1929
　Place: Folkwang Museum, Essen, Germany
　Company: Folkwang-Tanztheater-Studio

Persephone
　Music: Igor Stravinsky
　Design: Andre Barsacq
　Date: April 30, 1934
　Place: Paris Opera, Paris, France
　Company: Ida Rubinstein

Persephone
　Music: Igor Stravinsky
　Design: Dominik Hartmann
　Date: April 16, 1955
　Place: Opera House, Düsseldorf, Germany

Persephone
　Music: Igor Stravinsky
　Design: Hein Heckroth
　Date: March 8, 1964
　Place: Opera House, Essen, Germany

Persisches Ballet
  Music: Egon Wellesz
  Design: Hein Heckroth
  Date: July, 1924
  Place: Donaueschinger Musiktage, Germany
  Company: Neue Tanzbühne

Petrouchka
  Music: Igor Stravinsky
  Design: Hein Heckroth
  Date: February, 1930
  Place: Opera House, Essen, Germany
  Company: Folkwang-Tanztheater-Studio

Phasen/Phases
  Libretto: Kurt Jooss
  Music: Erich Sehlbach
  Design: Hermann Markard
  Date 1966
  Place: Stadthalle Mülheim, Germany
  Company: Folkwangballett

Polovetzer Tänze
  Music: Alexander Borodin
  Design: Hein Heckroth
  Date: November 1930
  Place: Opera House, Essen, Germany
  Company: Folkwang Tanzbühne Essen

Der verlorene Sohn/The Prodigal Son
  Music: Prokofiev
  Design: Hein Heckroth
  Date: May 28, 1931
  Place: Opera House, Essen, Germany
  Company: Folkwang Tanzbühne Essen

The Prodigal Son/Der verlorene Sohn
  Libretto: Kurt Jooss
  Music: Fritz A. Cohen
  Design: Hein Heckroth
  Date: October 6, 1933
  Place: Stadschouwburg, Amsterdam, Holland
  Company: Ballets Jooss

The Prodigal Son/Der verlorene Sohn
  Libretto: Kurt Jooss
  Music: Fritz A. Cohen
  Design: Dimitri Bouchèbe
  Date: October 1939
  Place: Prince's Theatre, Bristol, England
  Company: Ballets Jooss

The Prodigal Son/Der verlorene Sohn
  Libretto: Kurt Jooss
  Music: Fritz A. Cohen
  Design: Dominik Hartmann
  Date: May 23, 1955
  Place: Opera House, Düsseldorf, Germany

Der verlorene Sohn/The Prodigal Son
  Libretto: Kurt Jooss
  Music: Fritz A. Cohen
  Design: Dominik Hartmann
  Date: May 23, 1956
  Place: Opera House, Düsseldorf, Germany

Pulcinella
  Music: Igor Stravinsky
  Design: Hein Heckroth
  Date: April, 1932
  Place: Opera House, Essen, Germany
  Company: Folkwang Tanzbühne Essen

Rappresentazione di anima e di corpo
  Music: Emilio del Cavalieri
  Design: Veniero Colosanti/John Moore
  Date: 1968
  Place: Salzburger Festspiele
  Under the Direction of: Herbert Graf

Seltsammes Septett
  Libretto: Kurt Jooss
  Design: Sigurd Leeder
  Date: 1928
  Place: Opera House, Essen, Germany
  Company: Folkwang-Tanztheater-Studio

Seven Heroes/Die sieben Schwaben
  Libretto: Kurt Jooss
  Music: Henry Purcell (arranged by Fritz A. Cohen)
  Date: October 1, 1933
  Place: Schouwburg Maastricht, Holland
  Company: Ballets Jooss

Seven Heroes/Die sieben Schwaben
  Libretto: Kurt Jooss
  Music: Henry Purcell (arranged by Fritz A. Cohen)
  Design: Hein Heckroth
  Date: October 9, 1937
  Place: Lyric Theatre, Baltimore, USA
  Company: Ballets Jooss

Die Brautfahrt/A Spring Tale
 Libretto: Kurt Jooss
 Music: Jean-Philippe Rameau/Francois Couperin
 Design: Hein Heckroth
 Date: May 1925
 Place: Municipal Theatre, Münster, Germany
 Company: Neue Tanzbühne

A Spring Tale/Die Brautfahrt
 Libretto: Kurt Jooss
 Music: Fritz A. Cohen
 Design: Hein Heckroth
 Date: February 8, 1939
 Place: New Theatre, Oxford, England
 Company: Ballets Jooss

Suite 1929
 Libretto: Kurt Jooss
 Music: Fritz A. Cohen
 Design: Hein Heckroth
 Date: October 1929
 Place: Opera House, Essen, Germany
 Company: Folkwang-Tanztheater-Studio

Tanz-Suite
 Libretto: Kurt Jooss
 Music: Ernst Toch
 Design: Hein Heckroth
 Date: 1924
 Place: Municipal Theatre, Münster, Germany
 Company: Neue Tanzbühne

Tragodie
 Libretto: Kurt Jooss
 Music: Fritz A. Cohen
 Design: Hein Heckroth
 Date: May 1926
 Place: Municipal Theater, Münster, Germany
 Company: Neue Tanzbühne

Zimmer Nr. 13
 Libretto: Kurt Jooss
 Music: Fritz A. Cohen
 Design: Hein Heckroth
 Date: October 1929
 Place: Opera House, Essen, Germany
 Company: Folkwang-Tanztheater-Studio

Chorevgraphy and Dance
1993, Vol 3, Part 2, pp. 103-104
Photocopying permitted by license only

Notes on Contributors

Christian Holder was born in Trinidad, West Indies, and moved to London, England with his family as a small child. He made his performing debut there at the age of three with his father's group of Caribbean dancers. He began studying classical ballet privately at the age of seven and a few years later he joined the Corona Academy Stage School in London. A scholarship from Martha Graham brought him to the United States. Here he also enrolled at the High School of Performing Arts. At the school he was spotted by Robert Joffrey who invited him to join his company in 1966. He was a member of the Joffrey Ballet for thirteen years. As a soloist he worked with many distinguished choreographers including Massine, Robbins, Ailey, de Mille and Kurt Jooss. He has created many ballets of his own, most recently a piece called *Coup d'Estoc* based on the novel *Les Liasons Dangereuses*. Mr. Holder has also appeared in repertory theater productions, musicals and he designs wardrobes for the stage.

Anna Markard, daughter of Kurt Jooss, was born in Essen, Germany in 1931 and grew up in England. She began her professional dance training with Sigurd Leeder in London. She received additional training in modern dance at the Folkwangschule (Essen) and in classical ballet (Paris) and danced with the ballet company of the Düsseldorf Opera House. She has taught at the Folkwangschule, where she helped build and coach the Folkwang Ballet. In close collaboration with her father before his death, she reconstructed and staged the four works in the current Jooss repertory. Since 1971 she has set these works for companies all over the world and given lecture demonstrations and workshops in European modern dance. She lives in Amsterdam, Holland with her husband, the painter and designer Hermann Markard.

Susanne Schlicher studied Theatre and German Literature at the Universities of Cologne and Vienna, and received the Doctorate in 1984. She worked as an assistant producer with Hans Kresnik, a leading proponent of the West German Tanztheatre. At present Ms. Schlicher teaches at the University of Bremen and is artistic co-director of the German Dance Film Institute. She has lectured throughout Germany and in Italy, Belgium, Canada and the United States. In 1991 she was an invited lecturer on dance at the Theatre Department of the University of Giessen, Germany. Her book "Tanz-Theater" was published in 1987 by Rowohlt-Verlag and an Italian edition followed in 1989.

Walter Sorell was born in Vienna, Austria, in 1905, and emigrated to he United States in 1939. Book author, essayist, critic, dramatist, poet and painter, he was Associate Professor at Columbia University, and Barnard College (1954–1964); Hunter College (1966–1968); The New School (1954–1964); guest lectured at several universities and colleges in the States. He was principle dance critic for *Dance News*, contributing editor to *Dance Observer* and *Dance Scope*, drama editor and critic for *The Cresset*. He is author of twenty books, three plays and translated seven books from German into English. Among his best known books are: *The Dance Through the Ages, Dance in its Time, Looking Back in Wonder, The Mary Wigman Book* and *Hanya Holm: The Biography of an Artist*. Professor Sorell received the Dance Magazine Award of Distinction in 1985, and was honored by the Austrian Government bestowing upon him "Das Ehrenkreuz Erster Klausse fur Wissenschaft und Kunst" in 1991. His paintings have been exhibited at many galleries here and in Europe. Presently Professor Sorell is completing an autobiography which will appear in both English and German.

Suzanne K. Walther was born in Budapest, Hungary and entered the United States in 1957 as a refugee of the Hungarian revolution. She has a B.A. degree in Anthropology from the University of Hawaii and M.A. and Ph.D. degrees in Dance from New York University. The topic of her doctoral dissertation was Kurt Jooss. She has taught dance technique and dance related academic courses at Cedar Crest College and the United Nations Recreational Council. She was the dance columnist for the *Sunday Call-Chronicle*, and her reviews and articles have been published in several other newspapers and journals. She continues to study classical ballet with Vladimir Dokoudovsky. The two papers in this issue are taken in part from her forthcoming books on Kurt Jooss, which will be published by Gordon and Breach, Harwood Academic Publishers.

Choreography and Dance
1993, Vol 3, Part 2, pp. 105-108
Photocopying permitted by license only

Index

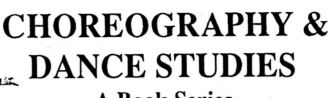

THE LANGUAGE OF DANCE SERIES

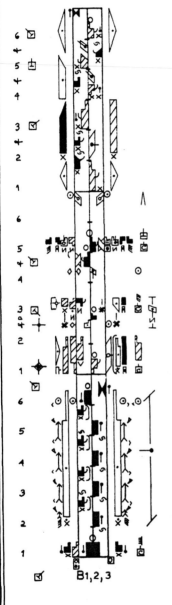

B1, 2, 3

Series Editors:
Ann Hutchinson Guest, Director of the Language of Dance Centre, London, UK
Ray Cook, Vassar College, New York, USA

The Language of Dance Series provides direct access to great masterpieces of dance through Labanotation. Each volume consists of the Labanotated score, historical background and study and performance notes for a specific dance. It aims to preserve original choreography, to enhance contemporary performance of the dances and to increase the appreciation of these international dance classics.

NEW!

Volume 5
SOKOLOW'S *BALLADE*
Edited by **Ray Cook**
June 1993 • 151pp • Softcover ISBN: 2-88124-913-2

Volume 4
TUDOR'S *SOIRÉE MUSICALE*
By **Ann Hutchinson Guest**
April 1993 • 106pp • Softcover ISBN: 2-88124-884-5 •
Hardcover ISBN: 2-88124-911-6

Previous titles...

Volume 3 **Nijinsky's** *Faune* Restored
1991 • 204pp • Softcover ISBN: 2-88124-819-5
Volume 2 **Shawn's** *Fundamentals of Dance*
1988 • 108pp • Softcover ISBN: 2-88124-219-7
Volume 1 **Bournonville's** *Pas de Deux* from
The Flower Festival in Genzano
1987 • 48pp • Softcover ISBN:2-88124-145-X

For further details, please contact:
Gordon and Breach Publishers
STBS Order Dept., PO Box 90, Reading, Berks. RG1 8JL, UK
Tel: *orders* (0734) 568316/*enquiries* (071) 836 5125 *or*
PO Box 786, Cooper Station, New York NY 10276, USA
Tel: orders (800) 545 8398/*enquiries* (212) 243 4411/4543
Fax: *UK* (0734) 568211 *or USA* (212) 645 2459

Printed in the United Kingdom
by Lightning Source UK Ltd.
129976UK00006B/18/A

9 783718 654482